Internal Audit Reports
Post Sarbanes-Oxley

Internal Audit Reports Post Sarbanes-Oxley

A Guide to Process-Driven Reporting

Susan Switzer

John Wiley & Sons, Inc.

For general information on our other products and services, or technical support, please contact our Customer Care Department within the United States at 800-762-2974, outside the United States at 317-572-3993 or fax 317-572-4002.

Wiley also publishes its books in a variety of electronic formats. Some content that appears in print may not be available in electronic books.

For more information about Wiley products, visit our Web site at http://www.wiley.com.

Library of Congress Cataloging-in-Publication Data:

Switzer, Susan, 1945-
  Internal audit reports post Sarbanes-Oxley : a guide to process-driven reporting / Susan Switzer.
      p. cm.
  Includes bibliographical references and index.
  ISBN: 978-0-470-05084-2 (cloth : alk. paper)
  1. Auditing, Internal--United States. 2. United States. Sarbanes-Oxley Act of 2002. I. Title.
  HF5616.U5S95 2007
  657'.4580973--dc22
                                    2006023999

10 9 8 7 6 5 4 3 2 1

CONTENTS

Preface   *vii*

Acknowledgments   *xi*

About the Author   *xiii*

About the Institute of Internal Auditors   *xiv*

SECTION ONE: FROM VENI, VIDI, VICI TO SOX   1

CHAPTER 1
Process-Driven Reporting   5

CHAPTER 2
The Latest Standards   25

CHAPTER 3
New Rules and New Tools   43

SECTION TWO: GOING WITH THE FLOW   55

CHAPTER 4
New Looks for Audit Reports   57

CHAPTER 5
The Value-Added Spoken (and E-Mailed) Word   76

SECTION THREE: REPORT WRITING 101, ER, MAKE THAT 404   **91**

CHAPTER 6
Critical Word Choices   95

CHAPTER 7
Structured Sentences   113

CHAPTER 8
Paragraphs, Punctuation, and Capitalization   129

CHAPTER 9
Graphics and Editing   140

SECTION FOUR: IT'S A FLAT WORLD AFTER ALL   **149**

CHAPTER 10
It's a Flat World After All   151

APPENDICES   **165**

APPENDIX A
Professional Standards   167

APPENDIX B
Find the Flaws   222

APPENDIX C
Bibliography   229

Index   231

PREFACE

From foots and ticks to dots and coms, internal auditors have witnessed and communicated headline-producing changes in the way business is conducted around the world.

Twenty-first-century auditors continue to serve as front-line reporters for what is happening; they are the knowledgeable insiders who amass and analyze financial and operational data, synthesize what they observe, and articulate their findings. And the recommendations they make serve as guideposts to keep business executives and audit committees fully informed—and out of jail.

In the wake of Sarbanes-Oxley, internal audit reports—the primary mode of communication—are more important than ever. In addition to being carefully organized and crisply written, reports need to connect the financial dots and relate specialized chunks of information to each other, to any potential risk, and to the company's overall operations and governance. Increasing automation and outsourcing also make it imperative that those dots are systematically connected.

The reports need to adhere to the same process that governs the audit itself. Process-driven reporting will make the difference between core dumps of data and well-structured reports that precisely point out the relationships between findings, conclusions, and recommendations—the kind of reports financial executives can attest to with confidence.

In this book, Chief Executive Officers and Chief Financial Officers, Audit Committee members, Chief Audit Executives, Controllers, Chief Information Officers, external auditors, accounting professors and students, and anyone involved in corporate audits will find up-to-the-minute methods for establishing effective internal audit report processes—and maybe even a little inspiration. And auditors whose second, third, or fourth language is English will be given practical tips on American business usage—plus the short list of what constitutes grammatical correctness.

Advances in information technology (IT) have added another significant component to the scope of internal audits; how corporate data are captured and made secure is a relatively new area of controls that must be examined. The good news is that similar advances in communication technology make many of these new issues less cumbersome. In fact, automated reports are fast becoming the state-of-the-art. IT as it relates to "New Rules and New Tools" is the hot topic of Chapter 3.

Internal Audit Reports Post Sarbanes-Oxley offers best practices in communicating what is observed during the audit process so that managers and executives can understand a company's financial infrastructures, internal controls, and potential risks as well as the auditors do.

To communicate effectively in the twenty-first century, a disciplined writing process, as carefully planned as the audit process, should be followed, no matter what form audit reports take and no matter how much of the reporting is automated. That process constitutes the core of this book and is described in four sections.

The first section, *From Veni, Vidi, Vici to SOX,* starts with the most basic step, deciding what to say, and Chapter 1 defines and illustrates process-driven reporting. Chapter 2 enumerates the various professional standards—from IIA and AICPA standards to principles of readability—that should be considered in saying what needs to be said. And Chapter 3, as mentioned, deals with IT, both the pluses and the minuses.

Section Two, *Going with the Flow,* further delineates the report writing process and integrates it with the audit process. Templates are included in Chapter 4, and the value-added aspects of spoken communication and e-mail are reviewed in Chapter 5.

Report Writing 101, Er, Make That 404 is the title of Section Three. Accordingly, Chapters 6 through 9 cover various practices that make words meaningful and turn information into knowledge—all in the context of the post–Sarbanes-Oxley generation of internal audit reports. Not every grammar rule and point of punctuation is covered, just the ones most likely to be useful to internal auditors. This section proceeds cumulatively, from individual words and sentences to paragraphs, graphics, and editing; examples of everything from precise verbs and well-placed modifiers to topic sentences and effective transitions are plentiful. In addition to time-saving techniques for writing and editing, tips on thinking more inclusively about the audit process are also included. The report is, after all, an organic outgrowth of the fieldwork— not a discrete and odious obstacle to be overcome!

The final section, *It's a Flat World After All,* deals with topics related to worldwide internal audit reporting, such as setting the right tone for diverse readers, analyzing the needs of multiple audiences, listening to and understanding what is expected in any culture, and writing about varied currencies. Antidotes to writer's block are also included.

Making information easy to access is always essential; therefore, this book offers handy checklists, *Samples and Examples,* and other useable chunks of instant information. Appendix B even includes some Find-the-Flaw exercises to test your GQ (Grammar Quotient). Highlighted sections of *Tips and Techniques* clarify the subjects being covered and offer material to "make your own." The popular tradition of borrowing from previous reports is only practical if well-written reports are used—so if sample phrases in this book can be fleshed out with specifics and used in a real-world, real-time time audit, be my guest!

In addition, you will find informative *Perspectives* about what is different since Sarbanes-Oxley and about what works and what doesn't— from international financial executives, internal audit executives, audit professionals in the academic world, IT wizards, and internal auditors, representing a variety of industries.

To all the observant, detail-oriented, and dedicated internal auditors telling the story of commerce as it unfolds—and to all the company executives who are working to achieve sustainable operations, manage risk, and exercise good governance—I say, three cheers!

This book will make your report writing—and reading—more satisfying.

Susan Switzer
January 2007

ACKNOWLEDGMENTS

Front-line acknowledgments go to the seminar participants from around the world with whom I have had the pleasure of working for the past two decades. Their commitment to their work and their competence with numbers—and language—have inspired me.

This book could not have been written without the help of Professor Richard Brody, Anderson Schools of Management, University of New Mexico; Steve Newstead, RubinBrown; and William Markel and Amy M. Finney, Crowe Chizek and Company LLC. Their willingness to contribute and advise during busy season was especially appreciated. And while the guidance was expert, any mistakes or misinterpretations are mine.

I would also like to acknowledge the valuable insights contributed by Stephane Girard, Schlumberger Ltd.; Ted Senko, KPMG; Robert E. Lefton, Ph.D., Psychological Associates, Inc.; Sanjay Gupta, Dionex; Thomas D. Zweifel, Ph.D., The Swiss Consulting Group; Joe Nici, The Movado Group; B.L. Jeffery, Systems Programmer; Bruce Fortelka, Kanbay International; Jasvir Gill, SAP; Liz Alhand, Texas Medical Center; Anand Adya and Aparna Deshpande, Greenlight Technologies; Bill Stevens, BBI Group; and Irv Diamond, Audit Committee Chair.

Other individuals contributed significant professional input and personal support during the research and writing of this book: Patricia D. Bender, Robert Bergeron, Beth Bindert, Ann Brooks, Jim Castellano, Nick Causton, Rick Corcoran, Joanna Corti, D.O.M, Debbie Craig,

Deborah A. Dacey, Bill Drake, Ahava Goldman, Jim Hamill, Patrick Horton, Ph.D., Ingrid Kelley, Ken Kiesler, Tom Lam, Robert Leggat, Cate Lochead, Sally Mahe, Paul Mansfield, Janis McCracken, Camilla McLaughlin, Stan Mengwasser, Melissa Murphy, Shirley Nguyen, Jim Oliver, Janet Orsak, Heidi Petersen, Frances Poteet, Deborah A. Primiano, Lois Purvis, Michael Ragsdale, Judith Sherinsky, Andy Smith, John Stephens, Jim Stolze, Claudia Suen, Sara Switzer, Edi Volvo, Lay Wilde, and Patsy Zurovec.

Special recognition goes to information designer Katie Ackerly, for the Combined Audit Process illustration, the flowcharts, and the sentence schemata. Ms. Ackerly has worked as an information mapper with The Grove Consultants International, holds a B.A. in Geosciences from Williams College, and is currently a researcher at the American Council for an Energy-Efficient Economy.

And the enthusiastic support of my editor, Timothy Burgard, and all the staff at John Wiley & Sons, Inc., is deeply appreciated.

Heartfelt thanks to all.

ABOUT THE AUTHOR

Susan Switzer has designed and conducted corporate communication seminars for the past 20 years. She is the former Director of Communications for KPMG/St. Louis and served on the firm's Executive Education faculty. She has a B.A. in English Literature from Manhattanville College, Purchase, New York, and an M.A. in Space Systems Management from Webster University, Colorado Springs.

ABOUT THE INSTITUTE OF INTERNAL AUDITORS

The Institute of Internal Auditors (IIA) is the primary international professional association, organized on a worldwide basis, dedicated to the promotion and development of the practice of internal auditing. The IIA is the recognized authority, chief educator, and acknowledged leader in standards, education, certification, and research for the profession worldwide. The Institute provides professional and executive development training, educational products, research studies, and guidance to more than 80,000 members in more than 100 countries. For additional information, visit the Web site at *www.theiia.org*.

FROM VENI, VIDI, VICI TO SOX

Veni, Vidi, Vici.

Julius Caesar

Reports, in one form or other, are part of human history. Julius Caesar, who is often credited for conciseness, simply declared: "I came, I saw, I conquered," which, in the original Latin, is even shorter: *Veni, Vidi, Vici*. However, if Caesar had written his report after Sarbanes-Oxley (SOX), those words might have been questioned, and they probably would have been generated by computer software.

Twenty-first-century internal auditors face a whole new set of challenges as they carry out their professional duty to "communicate the engagement results."[1] The reports required by SOX deal with primarily internal control issues and are not the same as the traditional financial and operations audit reports. But since SOX, all reports written by internal auditors are being more closely scrutinized—by Audit Committees, management, and the external auditors who review their work.

While oral reports are still permissible for interim reporting, the tangible document form has become generally accepted as the best method of delivering the goods produced by the internal audit function—whether traditional or SOX-related. Without some sort of synthesis of what was observed during the audit, executives conceivably would need to reexamine all of the data the auditors covered in order to attest to their company's financial condition or adequacy of internal controls. We can live without that kind of system redundancy! The current challenges for Chief Audit Executives (CAEs) and internal auditors involve finding effective ways to collaborate throughout the process and to communicate audit findings in a regulatory environment characterized by controls transformation and new legislative requirements. Collaboration and communication skills are themes throughout this book, as are techniques for "connecting the dots."

Chapter 1, "Process-Driven Reporting," defines the audit report writing process as an integrated component of the audit—and explores the most critical step in that process: deciding what to say. In its simplest terms, this decision has always been driven by the general audit objective of alerting management to potential risk. Now, since SOX, the mandate to categorize (i.e., likelihood, frequency, materiality) and connect those risks to specific situations and systems must be followed. In fact, serving as facilitators for Enterprise Risk Management (ERM) is perceived as one of the internal audit function's new communication missions.[2]

Differences in the reporting process mandated by SOX are the subject of Chapter 2, which includes *Perspectives* from internal audit executives and software developers on the report-relevant implications of some of the new regulations and directives. "The Latest Standards" also reviews current professional standards that have implications for internal audit reporting. In the interest of saving time and focusing on essentials, excerpts from only the most directly applicable standards are presented. More complete selections of internal audit–related standards from the Institute of Internal Auditors (IIA), Sarbanes-Oxley (SOX) legislation, Public Company Accounting Oversight Board (PCAOB), and framework of the Committee of Sponsoring Organizations of the Treadway Commission (COSO) are contained in Appendix A.

Chapter 3, "New Rules and New Tools," examines Information Technology (IT) tools now available for the report production process—and how they relate to SOX requirements. *Tips and Techniques* for successfully articulating IT issues—and dealing with IT problems—are also provided. Given the anticipated arrival of fully automated reporting, ways to successfully communicate in a digitally driven auditing environment are examined, and *Perspectives* from IT executives are presented.

Notes

1. The Institute of Internal Auditors, *International Standards for the Professional Practice of Internal Auditing, Section 2400-Communicating Results,* 2004.
2. K.H. Spencer Pickett, *Audit Planning: A Risk-Based Approach* (Hoboken, NJ: John Wiley & Sons, 2006).

CHAPTER I

PROCESS-DRIVEN REPORTING

Writing, like auditing, is a systematic process. Contrary to popular myths about wild-eyed literary celebrities—and widely held perceptions that math and verbal skills are mutually exclusive—writing is a lot like computer programming, especially report writing.

REPORT WRITING AS PROGRAMMING

Like programming, report writing is going after something: a conclusion to be reached and acted on, a successful delivery of information, a new set of results or outputs to be acknowledged. Creating an "A-ha!" moment for Audit Committees, Chief Audit Executives (CAEs), and managers, similar to what programmers experience when the data runs successfully against the software they have written, is something for internal auditors to aspire to when writing reports.

Report writing also proceeds logically, from one step to the next, including whatever supports the thesis and discarding whatever is unnecessary or distracting. Anyone who has ever watched a computer program "loop" understands the importance of proceeding systematically from A to B to C, without skipping B. And anyone whose manager has ever fired back a red-lined draft of an internal audit report knows that including only relevant content is an absolute requirement.

Like effective programming, effective report writing also stands the tests of time, multiple users, and multiple interpretations. Screenwriters call that quality "making lines actor-proof"; internal auditors might call it "making causal relationships transparent." Although people often interpret the same words differently, it is possible to write so that most of the readers will be in consensus—at least about the most important points, and at least the most important readers.

A typical programming flowchart begins at the starting point oval and goes on to include rectangles indicating activities, diamonds representing decision points, and curled-edge boxes showing document output. Using those same symbols, a Generic Audit Process flowchart is shown in Exhibit 1.1. The terminology will differ depending on whether the audit is a Sarbanes and Oxley (SOX) audit or a traditional financial or operations audit; however, the same logical process applies.

The Audit Process begins with a request for an audit, or notification of one, and proceeds through various activity steps. Each step—whether it comprises the formal audit conference, fieldwork planning meetings, on-site controls testing, status briefings, completion and review of work papers, high-priority e-mails requesting access to additional files, or conversations with managers, CAEs, or audit committee members—involves communication. Much of that communication is written.

The Report Writing Process also begins with the notification of an audit. The written report is not a separate task to be tacked on—and tackled—after the real work has been accomplished. Data gathering for the report begins with the first documents that refer to that particular audit, and the mental work of writing begins then as well. To save time at the end, start thinking about the report from the beginning.

Each of the steps in the Report Writing Process flowchart (see Exhibit 1.2) directly reflects the activities of the audit process; in fact, some are identical.

EXHIBIT 1.1 *Generic Audit Process*

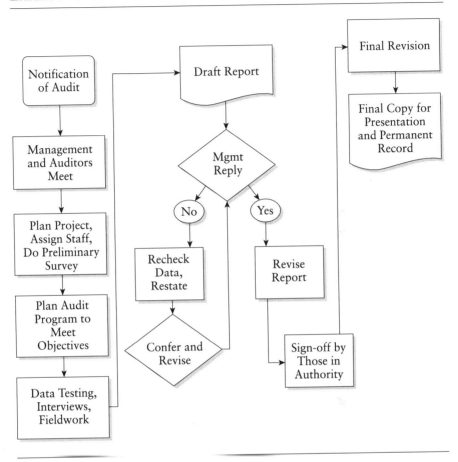

A flowchart for the Comprehensive Audit Reporting Process is shown in Exhibit 1.3.

Before describing the seven steps, a quick look at the process as a whole is in order.

PROCESS-DRIVEN REPORTING DEFINED

Process-driven reporting is not really new; however, the emphasis on process—that is, looking at the path taken by information through a

EXHIBIT 1.2 *Report Writing Process*

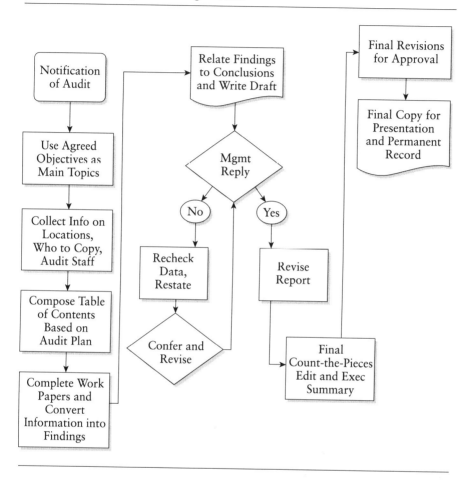

company—as opposed to just the information itself, has not been valued in the business world until recently.

Tracing the progress of information from controls testing to conclusion in an audit report was not as crucial either—until pointing out the relationship between such elements as missing files and overstated earnings became critical. This need for closer, connect-the-dots risk assessment was mandated by SOX, but for many companies, process-driven reporting has been in place for some time.

EXHIBIT 1.3 *Comprehensive Audit Reporting Process*

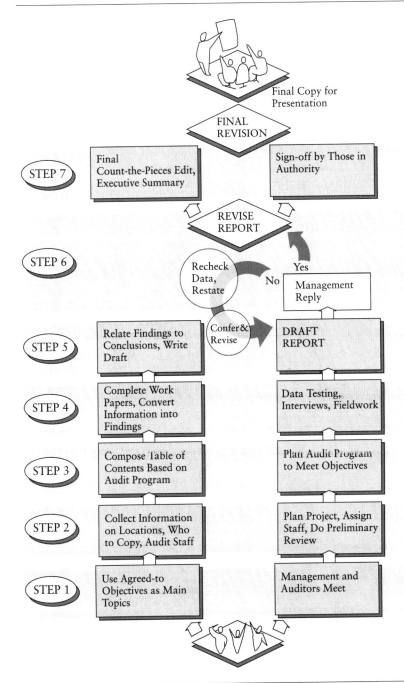

Any process is simply a methodology made up of continuing developments or iterations—a particular way of doing something comprising different steps. Subsequent steps depend on what occurred in the preceding steps. Therefore, noticing what happens, responding to changes, and articulating the progression between the steps is critical. Vivek Ranadive talks about "event-driven companies" that "manage by exception."[1] In these organizations, changes are noticed and responded to—in real time. Such organizations possess "the technical structure to deliver integrated, real-time, active information and the human culture to transform information into knowledge and then into informed, ongoing action."[2] An internal audit report does that too: transforms information into knowledge and, by means of the recommendations, into informed, ongoing action.

Process-driven reporting also depends on—and SOX requires—collaboration. Audit professionals in any company who rarely communicate directly with each other (anyone who sends e-mails to the next cubicle, tune in on this one!) can lose perspective about what is happening in terms of financial operations or internal controls. But when audit committee members, management, and auditors have the opportunity to discuss issues together, there is less likelihood of distortion in the conclusions, and more opportunity for communicating complete and accurate engagement results.

Computer Sciences Corporation executives commented on post-SOX guidance from the Securities and Exchange Commission (SEC) and Public Company Accounting Oversight Board (PCAOB) saying they hoped it would enable auditors to "realign their audit scope and refocus their procedures." They said: "Moreover, enhanced planning and coordination between issuers and their auditors, as well as acceleration of issuer testing for higher risk areas, should have resulted in improved audit integration, expanded reliance and significantly lower fees."[3]

On the subject of effective planning, the Audit Committee Chair of a national bank insists that internal auditors report to the committee without any filtering by management. He believes in setting the work plan and scope of each audit in conjunction with the internal auditors, be they in-house or outsourced, and characterizes the current audit reporting climate as one of greater diligence and communication. "Meetings are also much better documented since Sarbanes-Oxley," he said.[4]

From a report-writing perspective, those carefully kept minutes can serve as reliable guideposts for the actual report—preventive rewrite, we might say. In terms of production, this type of process-driven internal audit report is a seamless and logical outgrowth of the audit work instead of an isolated chore. It is easier to write and more satisfying to read.

THE COMPREHENSIVE AUDIT REPORTING PROCESS

An analysis of each of the seven steps in the comprehensive audit reporting process follows. Each step spotlights a particular communication skill, such as listening or linking, but all of the skills are applicable in all of the steps.

Step 1: Listening and Interpreting

The first meeting establishes relationships that will carry through the entire audit; therefore, listening skills are essential. When the expectations for a particular audit are initially stated—via a formal Terms of Reference (TOR) document, a discussion about intended objectives, or a listing of areas of greatest potential risk—it pays to pay attention. Productive listening, sometimes called active listening, means paying such close attention that, with respect to anticipated outcomes and audit objectives, the internal auditor can restate what is being asked following the meeting, and the CAE and audit committee members all agree.

Sometimes internal auditors sit through the formal audit conference and only hear what is said—without really listening. If that sounds like mumbo-jumbo, listen up. Active listeners are open to what the Chief Financial Officer (CFO) or CAE is saying without trying to finish the thoughts themselves or prepare "I got it covered" responses. To put it another way, active listeners tune in to what is being broadcast and get the message loud and clear without creating static by starting to mentally plan their work. They are even taking a few notes that can be used as headings for the report.

LISTENING TIPS AND TECHNIQUES

If you wonder whether you are an active listener, ask yourself these five questions:

1. Do you let speakers finish without interruption?
2. Can you prevent distractions from disrupting your listening?
3. Can you tolerate silence and let the speakers collect their thoughts?
4. Do you notice body language and incorporate it into the message being delivered?
5. Do you ask questions to clarify and amplify what was said?

If you can answer yes to all five questions, congratulations! And keep listening.

Optimum communication will occur when the assigned audit staff can attend even the initial meetings with the audit sponsor. CAEs and managers pass on the best information they have, but any time information is transmitted and distributed among many people, there is a chance that certain nuances of meaning will be lost—or altered.

Interpretations Differ—Be Specific

Every person interprets information differently. Even people working together in the same company who have the same objectives and speak the same language will infer different meanings from the same set of words.

The following data definition mantra is useful for both auditors and Information Technology (IT) people: "To accurately roll up financial data, it is imperative that the data have unambiguous definitions."[5]

In Step 1, many companies use audit request forms of one type or another to pinpoint the scope of the audit or areas of the business to be examined. Categories on a typical audit request form might include

Situation and Reasons for Project, Description of Project and Objectives, and Work and Final Products Requested. Other report headings might be even more direct: the Existing Situation, the Should-Be Condition, and the Effects on Costs and Performance. One post-SOX report format simply includes Project Scope and Objectives, Executive Summary, and Opportunities for Improvement.

Whichever set of categories is selected, being as specific as possible at this stage of the process sets an important precedent, one that will pay off later. Immediacy carries energy. The words used to describe a tricky issue, such as valuation of fixed assets, when that issue is first brought forward are likely to be used later. To avoid getting stuck with abstract generalities then, write down exactly what is said using quantifiable terms—in real time.

An agreed-upon audit plan also provides the necessary elements for the report's Table of Contents (TOC), and the TOC can then serve as a reference point for determining essential information throughout the course of the audit.

Step 2: Collaborating on Audit Components

Since SOX, making collaborative decisions about the audit plan is not only beneficial, but necessary. Step 2, which involves assigning the audit team, planning fieldwork, determining the distribution list, and other administrative specifics, is an excellent place to practice collaboration skills.

Collaboration is important at all stages of the process, but most especially, when the groundwork for the audit is being established. Internal auditors should make a point of conferring with their CAE, audit committee, and managers together. That way, hot topics such as revenue recognition can be clarified, and any other potentially ambiguous terms can be defined before they appear in a report that then requires too many revisions.

Any relevant background—not all the background, just what is required—can be researched and written up during this step, such as the name of the entity and description of the business, the purpose of the audit, and what the areas of concentration (read "highest risk") should be.

An understanding of the business—and the businesspeople—being audited cannot be underestimated. Auditors may be so intent on strictly following professional guidelines that they, justifiably, omit reviewing a procedure such as payroll and expenses (P&E), but if the CEO wants to know those details, the P&E audit stays in the picture.

Knowing what the audience wants, what all the audiences want, is essential. As more and more auditing work is outsourced, conducting a little informal market research to determine what is desired is critical. Ask the audit committee what they want.

Sometimes asking for what we want is not as easy as it sounds. We have all attended luncheons where the salt or the salad dressing is across the table, and the person seated there is engaged in conversation with somebody important. When it comes to setting the parameters for an audit, do not hesitate to ask for the salt. Information about how to effectively probe is contained in Chapter 5.

The Components

Many internal audit departments are revising the classic five audit components, whittling them down to three or four, or shifting the emphasis to risk-related components. The Institute of Internal Auditors (IIA) does not specify five required components, but, with respect to disclosing noncompliance, the performance standard is as follows:

> When noncompliance with the Standards impacts a specific engagement, communication of the results should disclose the Standard(s) with which full compliance was not achieved, Reasons for noncompliance, and Impact of noncompliance on the engagement.[6]

Standards, Reasons, and Impact are comparable to the classic components of Criteria, Causes, and Effects. The traditional five are listed in Exhibit 1.4.

EXHIBIT **1.4** *The Traditional Five Components*

Conditions: Problems or opportunities—plus evidence

Criteria: Applicable standards, policies, or procedures

Causes: Conditions, circumstances, practices, or fundamental weaknesses that allowed the conditions to occur

Effects: Cost, exposure, risk, or timeliness issues that are actual or potential effects of what was observed

Recommendations: What needs to be done to fix the problems and what the benefits will be

Step 3: Deciding Core Issues

Deciding the core issues to be covered in a particular audit is another step where listening and collaboration skills add value. In this third step, the fieldwork outline is refined into a precisely orchestrated program that will meet audit objectives. Management may have requested a review of X, but the auditors, who have been noticing Y, should suggest that the scope be enlarged to accommodate the latest data. This step should always be left open for new data and circumstances that arise.

Whether auditing traditional areas such as financial due diligence or conducting a formal SOX audit of internal controls and risk, internal auditors need to deepen their focus. Completing a checklist of line items for review is not enough; questions need to be asked regarding what matters in this specific situation, in this particular company. The IIA says: "Internal auditors should conduct a preliminary assessment of the risks relevant to the activity under review. Engagement objectives should reflect the results of this assessment."[7]

Deciding what matters, like deciding what to say, is essential in telling any story—and "story" here does not mean something that is not true. Story, in the context of business reporting, means getting the point across logically—without gaps—in a way that engages readers and makes meanings easier to grasp.

Like any good story, internal audit reports contain all the necessary narrative elements—findings to be acknowledged, recommendations to be dealt with, potential risks to be avoided, heroes and heroines, and an ending that promises sustainability and profitability. (Have the video game people gotten hold of this concept yet?) Positive endings are, naturally, what most financial executives are interested in; therefore, smart internal auditors start focusing on their conclusions from the beginning.

Current Criteria for Risk

Deciding what to say with regard to potential risk issues involves looking at a range of different criteria. What was once merely a matter of dollars—anything over a predetermined amount was material and therefore important—has become far more complex. For example, Michael Ramos distinguishes "design deficiencies" from "operating deficiencies," and notes that the SEC contrasts "significant deficiencies" (same as "reportable conditions" per the American Institute of Certified Public Accountants, AICPA) and "material weaknesses." The terms "likelihood" and "significance" must also be considered when deciding whether to include a finding of potential risk.[8]

Continual, and often undocumented, upgrades in IT technology, are also adding new criteria for the decision about what to say. Internal auditors are used to analyzing inventories and receivables, reviewing payrolls and personnel, and, more and more, understanding how the IT software works. Therefore, the connection can be made between how company activities are accounted for and what the probable outcome of those activities will be. At this step, the focus should be on information that will make it easiest for management to understand what actions must be taken to prevent fraud and protect against risk.

Step 4: Essentials versus Nonessentials

The main complaint audit directors and managers make about internal audit reports is that the auditors include too much information (TMI). The cry of TMI needs to be taken seriously! True, internal auditors examine a high volume of data, and it can be difficult to disengage from facts and figures that are fascinating, that necessitated time-consuming efforts, and that seem relevant at first analysis.

A truism regarding any kind of writing is: "You can't say everything without ending up saying nothing." Saying more than is necessary is generally more of a problem in internal audit report writing than withholding information.

Along with questions about structure, auditors with whom I have worked ask most often about how much information to include. Professor Richard Brody emphasizes the importance of focusing on the big picture and not getting bogged down in the details. He says: "From an IA perspective, any kind of problem may be worth noting. But situation-based decisions need to be made about the significance of each. The question to ask is: which issues are significant enough to bring up to the client? Then talk to the client and reach agreement that those are the areas that should be included. And, don't wait till the end of the job to communicate weaknesses."[9]

Successful internal auditors communicate with the managers upfront and get to know and understand the nature of their business and what their concerns are. Then, in addition to complying with IIA professional standards—and SOX requirements, if applicable—they report the specific conditions, causes, and recommendations that the decision makers and implementers need to know.

Suppose an operations audit requires a month-long study of inventory procedures and reveals more than 300 different discrepancies. Each has a unique set of circumstances, and one-third of them approach substantial materiality levels. To include all 300 cases in the report is tempting—a nice list in an embedded table at the end, perhaps? Especially when at least half of the cases required hours of high-level detective work and analysis to uncover. But all management really needs to know is that the software needs tweaking because an aggregate of X dollars is in question. A statement summarizing the situation that references the 300 cases and significant percentages will get the auditors the credit they deserve without drowning the managers in data.

Auditors do valuable work; however, reports are not the place to exhibit *all* of that work. Paradoxically, fewer words and lower page counts are what make reports value-added.

Different Foci for Different Folks

Different audits naturally call for different points of emphasis. The main message for a postacquisition report, for example, is whether the acquisition price was worth it—with specific references to the success of the integration of the new entity, whether projections were realistic and whether they were met, and whether sufficient legal, financial, and technical due diligence was carried out. For a routine financial report, the sponsors might be asked whether any unusual circumstances or anomalous events should be given special attention with regard to significant internal control issues. If the report is more of a management evaluation, then the main message should synthesize the overall functioning of the company—with specific examples. And for the newly mandated SOX reports, the theme is generally one of ranking observed and potential risks and connecting them to recommendations with clearly spelled-out consequences. All of the audit team members should keep an index card with the main message next to their computers and refer to it as they decide what to include in the report.

Series of Selections

Once the primary message decisions are made and agreed on, a series of judicious selections based on those messages is required.

On the macro level, if the internal auditor has not synthesized the major message of the report into two or three sentences, he or she will have a hard time producing a coherent report that can be summarized in a couple of pages and will most likely enumerate conditions and situations that are not relevant to the audit objective, and will utilize unnecessary words, draw unclear conclusions, and write run-on sentences—like this one! Managers who have to read such a report will have numerous questions and will want to make lots of changes.

Conversely, when auditors neatly sum up the message, they can then relate all supporting data to that message and write a conclusion that reinforces the message and their solid thinking—and satisfies SOX and every other professional standard. Professionals are valued for how they think more than for what they know. No matter how interested people are in a subject, the twenty-first-century business world of high volumes and low attention spans does not allow time for everything. Anyone who tries to say it all says nothing.

To those internal auditors who have managers or audit sponsors who *do* want to see it all: appendices and other extra-vehicular modules are the key. Tips on how to package information for detail-demanding readers are included in Chapter 9.

Create Categories

After compiling field notes and selecting the most effective supporting details from among all the data, create categories and subheadings based on those selections. It is not enough to list a series of discrepancies or misstatements or merely point out that X files are improperly controlled or supervised. A synthesizing statement about the condition that is indicated by those facts should be made.

Step 5: Linking and Synthesis Thinking

This is the step where a collection of data is transformed into a report, where what the auditors have been thinking gets expressed on the page. This is also where the communication skill of linking, or synthesis thinking, is used to relate the findings to the conclusions and to articulate the recommendations.

Categorized as a higher-order thinking skill (HOTS), synthesis thinking may be the only aspect of auditing that will not eventually be automated or outsourced. Synthesis thinking can be defined as the ability (1) to see patterns, organize parts, and identify components; (2) to generalize from given facts, relate knowledge from several areas, and draw conclusions; and (3) to compare and discriminate between ideas, make choices based on reasoned arguments, and verify the value of evidence.[10]

As auditors assemble data for a report, they are already engaged in the process of filing the information in their own internal computers. At the same time, they are noticing the relationships between the different data sets that are being filed. Linking, therefore, begins the moment the auditor walks into the audit site. As facts are gathered and aggregated, the thinking that accompanies those tasks is not only linear—that is, related to organizing the data for future reference—but the HOTS are also analytical and synthesizing. This thinking includes asking questions such as: How significant are these missing authorization signatures to overall internal controls? Is a lack of segregation of duties in this instance material to company operations? How does this tie to what the CEO and Audit Committee need to know?

Audit Committee Chair, Board Member, and BBI Group executive Bill Stevens says that since 2002, audit committees are required to be more rigorous in everything they do. "The committees are spending more time—the meetings are longer, there are more people in them, and more work is done between meetings," he said. "Being vigilant and staying on top of all financial operations, including internal controls, is an ongoing process."[11] But ultimately, the audit committee members only need to know the implications of all those inconsistent data entries; they should not have to read every one of them.

Changing Direction at Report Time

For the internal auditor, conclusions and recommendations are based on observed data, and the process is inductive, meaning it moves from amassing discrete items to a general summation. However, the written report requires the opposite approach. The team needs to change field direction, so to speak, when it comes time to structure a report that addresses the needs of the executive readers.

As opposed to the inductive method exemplified in the data-gathering part of the process, data synthesis calls for a deductive approach. The report should proceed from the conclusion, or general statement of the main message, to particular supporting data, including only as much of the latter as is absolutely necessary.

For example, if, after files are collected, reviewed, and analyzed, more than half are found to have been improperly handled, the conclusion is drawn that improved controls are needed. The written report would begin by stating that improved controls are needed, and then proceed to explain the basis of that recommendation. References to observed data can be arranged in MS Excel spreadsheets and charts of various kinds to make accessing the supporting data easier. The point is: Effective reports do not lead off with a list of specific instances in which controls were lacking. Executives and audit committees want to know what they need to take action on, and then they want to know the details.

Linking and Synthesis Thinking

Linking and synthesis thinking make it easier to reverse the particular-to-general audit logic flow and to connect the dots the way the report readers expect them to appear—general to particular. Furthermore, applying the skill of linking (PricewaterhouseCoopers calls it *connected-thinking*)[12] results in a document that CFOs and Audit Committees can (1) read quickly, (2) immediately relate to, and (3) trust to keep them fully informed.

Step 6: Rewrites and When to Quit

Step 6, identical in both the report writing process and the audit process, is usually composed of several iterations, because this step involves getting approvals on the wording of the document.

Even when people agree on the content, the temptation to change, alter, revise, improve, rewrite (you get the idea) another person's copy is irresistible. The first draft may not be in line with what management expected, conditions may have changed since the audit began, new information may have recently become available, or new management may have come on the scene. For whatever reason, this step usually takes some time, because revisions then need to be reviewed. And only when all are in agreement can the document be sent on to the final step. But these discussions and revisions are actually good for the final product; they add value. Invariably, either new information or a new take on the old information are brought forward during this part of the process.

All Good Writing Involves Rewriting

Furthermore, it is impossible to write a complete and satisfying report in one draft; professional writers would not even consider it. The craft of writing is actually rewriting. So, schedule time for the discussions, listen up, and enjoy the collaborative process.

One caveat: The tendency of some managers to overedit should be curbed—with or without enthusiasm. Ask those who edit to focus on finding factual inaccuracy rather than picking apart prepositional phrasing or punctuation, but get to know who is a stickler for what kind of wording—and act accordingly. Understand that most people, when asked to read a draft of any document, believe they have not done their job unless they find an error. Leaving in a few immaterial misspellings can often assuage that editorial need to locate something.

Step 7: Executive Summaries

The draft is approved, and the report is ready to go into production. Right? What about an Executive Summary? Paradoxically again, these summaries have gained in importance as they have decreased in length.

Most internal audit reports need an executive summary; having a shortened version of anything longer than 10 pages is insurance that the message will be delivered. For instance, one multinational company requires its internal auditors to write reports no longer than 20 pages, with a 2-page executive summary. In the case of the generally shorter SOX reports, however, readers are more likely to read the entire report.

Executive summaries can be written earlier in the process, but chances are that final, approved information will only be available at Step 7. In Audit Standard 3 on Audit Documentation, the PCAOB notes that: "Conclusions reached early on during an audit may be based on incomplete information or an incorrect understanding."[13] All the more reason to review, rethink, and revise.

As the summary is prepared, editing for consistency and overall appearance can take place. Comprehensive tips and techniques on editing are contained in Chapter 9, but the most important are to count the pieces, match the titles, make it look good, and read it aloud.

The results of this seven-step process? The final copy of the report is ready for presentation, distribution, and the permanent record. Not, we hope, for the evening news.

Notes

1. Vivek Ranadive, *The Power of Now* (New York: McGraw-Hill, 1999).
2. Ibid.
3. PCAOB/SEC Roundtable, May 10, 2006. Comments submitted by Leon J. (Lee) Level and Michael E. Keane, Computer Sciences Corporation, *www.sec.gov/news/press/4-511.shtml.*
4. Irv Diamond, Audit Committee Chair, telephone interview, March 2006.
5. Gwen Thomas, "SOX and the Database Professional: Mainframe Compliance Issues," *z/Journal*, October/November 2005.
6. From *Performance Standard 2430*. Copyright 2004 by The Institute of Internal Auditors, Inc., 247 Maitland Avenue, Altamonte Springs, Florida 32710-4210 U.S.A. Reprinted with permission.
7. From *Standards*, Section 2210.A1. Copyright 2004 by The Institute of Internal Auditors, Inc., 247 Maitland Avenue, Altamonte Springs, Florida 32710-4201 U.S.A. Reprinted with permission.
8. Michael Ramos, *How to Comply with Sarbanes-Oxley Section 404: Assessing the Effectiveness of Internal Control* (Hoboken, NJ: John Wiley & Sons, 2004).
9. Richard Brody, Ph.D., CPA, CFE, Anderson Schools of Management, University of New Mexico, telephone interview, March 2006.

10. D.R. Krathwohl, B.S. Bloom, and B.M. Bertram, *Taxonomy of Educational Objectives, the Classification of Educational Goals, Handbook II: Affective Domain* (New York: David McKay Co., 1973).
11. Bill Stevens, BBI Group, e-mail correspondence, May 2006.
12. PricewaterhouseCoopers, *www.pwcglobal.com.*
13. Public Company Accounting Oversight Board, Auditing Standard No. 3, Section 32.

CHAPTER 2

THE LATEST
STANDARDS

Internal auditors need to consider many new standards and directives as they produce the reports, both SOX-specific and traditional, that contribute to improved corporate governance—and keep executives fully informed.

The IIA, the foremost international professional association for internal auditors, says:

> Internal auditors have been confronted with a range of questions and issues related to their role and involvement in Sections 302 and 404 initiatives. These questions include both short-term issues during the implementation phase of reporting processes, as well as longer-term questions on the role and responsibilities of internal audit in this process.[1]

Accordingly, the IIA is establishing more inclusive standards in response to both the SOX legislation and subsequent directives from the various oversight agencies that protect the interests of investors. The IIA standards that most affect the report-writing process are reviewed in this chapter, followed by a look at some of the possible implications of SEC, PCAOB, and AICPA regulations and standards. How the COSO framework might relate to the report process is covered as well. While the IIA standards directly apply to internal auditors, much of the guidance from other agencies can also be profitably incorporated into the reporting process.

Now that the deadlines for SOX compliance are being met, the reality of putting that compliance into practice can use all the collective wisdom it can get. Other agency directives may help develop a clear picture of what "assessing the effectiveness of the internal control structure and procedures . . . for financial reporting"[2] looks like in the twenty-first century.

Many corporations and organizations that produce internal audit reports are also adding their own standards to the mix. This chapter, therefore, includes a look at company reporting standards. And, last but not least, readability standards are reviewed.

WHAT IS DIFFERENT SINCE SOX?

Before examining the various standards and their possible implications, here are comments from an international internal audit executive, a VP of internal controls, and a software entrepreneur about what they see as major differences in the reporting process since SOX.

PERSPECTIVE

Stephane Girard, Director of Internal Audit, Schlumberger Ltd., said: "SOX undoubtedly has brought more discipline into the process to remedy and close deficiencies identified by internal audit. For the audit department, this means streamlining the reporting process—often through IT applications—and speeding up the issuance of reports to provide time to re-test ineffective controls."

Joe Nici, Vice President of Business Controls for The Movado Group, said: "The most important change in the post-SOX era is the reaffirmation of the importance of management's responsibility for internal control. As a result, this responsibility naturally trickles down to all the employees in the organization and eventually becomes part of each employee's responsibility. Internal Audit is in a position to be well-respected in the organization because its specific internal control expertise can assist the organization's process owners in achieving their control responsibilities. ...My best advice to auditors is to keep in mind that their objectives and those of the company are aligned. A clear understanding of those common objectives—operational, financial, reporting, and compliance—will allow for a clear articulation of the risks associated with *not* achieving them. And internal auditors will be better accepted—and even appreciated."

Jasvir Gill, General Manager, Governance, Risk, and Compliance, SAP, had this to say: "Before the SOX legislation, people could plead ignorance. That is no longer possible. CFOs better make sure they know what is in their reports, and that it accurately reflects what is going on in their companies. Of course, the spirit of SOX should have been implemented all along, and, going forward, I believe audit committees and executives will understand this legislation as a friend. The SOX requirements can actually help companies build better controls—and with better controls, companies can better predict outcomes and thus improve their business."

IIA Standards

The IIA is the recognized authority of the internal audit profession, and the most recent *Standards* update notes that:

> Internal audit activities are performed in diverse legal and cultural environments; within organizations that vary in purpose, size, complexity, and structure; and by persons within or outside the organization.[3]

Such diversity brings energy to any enterprise, but also requires state-of-the-art communication skills, such as those enumerated in Chapter 1.

The IIA sets out its specific Criteria for Communicating in Section 2400:

> Communications should include the engagement's objectives and scope as well as applicable conclusions, recommendations and action plans.

> 2410.A1—Final communication of engagement results should, where appropriate, contain the internal auditor's overall opinion and or conclusions.

> 2410.A2—Internal auditors are encouraged to acknowledge satisfactory performance in engagement communications.

> 2410.A3—When releasing engagement results to parties outside the organization, the communication should include limitations on distribution and use of the results.

2410.C1—Communication of the progress and results of consulting engagements will vary in form and content depending upon the nature of the engagement and the needs of the client.[4]

With the exception of the distribution limitation, communication techniques for following those directives will be covered in subsequent chapters.

IIA Writing Standards

The IIA's seven criteria for *Quality of Communications* are reviewed in detail here.

Commonly understood terminology is crucial; therefore, a dictionary definition, courtesy of *Webster's New World Dictionary*, has been added to each of the criteria on the list:

1. *Accurate*: Careful and exact, free from mistakes or errors, precise, adhering closely to a standard.
2. *Objective*: Of or having to do with a known or perceived object as distinguished from something existing only in the mind of the subject or person thinking, real, actual, independent of the mind.
3. *Clear*: Free from confusion or ambiguity, not obscure, easily understood. (The word transparent comes to mind.)
4. *Concise*: Brief and to the point, short and clear.
5. *Constructive*: Leading to improvements or advances, formative, positive.
6. *Complete*: Full, whole, entire, brought to a conclusion.
7. *Timely*: Happening, done, said at a suitable time. (But the word "vague" comes to mind. Alternatives to "timely" are offered in Chapter 6.)

Writing by the Standards

A list of report-writing adjectives, even when defined, means something only when the methodology for producing such writing is understood. Here, therefore, are suggestions on how to write the way the IIA prescribes:

1. *Accuracy* should not be a problem for people who are trained to notice details, and much of the audited (and automated) information now can be transferred directly from existing files to the report. Regardless of the technology, note any significant information that is conveyed in conversation, ask for confirmation on e-mails, make sure you are getting through to IT professionals and others, and check that you have understood them. "Do my observations agree with yours?" "I heard you say..." "Please correct me if I'm wrong." Incorporating phrases like these into the audit process can save hours of argument and rewrites later. Or, if you are feeling particularly confident: "I might have missed something, so is there anything you want to add?"

2. *Objectivity* can be more difficult to achieve—or be perceived as having achieved. The best way to be considered objective is to declare only that which is quantifiable—that is, able to be actually observed and counted by somebody else. For example, no one can argue with: "Accounts Receivable was down USD 50,000 in the third quarter." However, if the sentence leads off with a non-quantifiable comment such as: "Because of inefficient accounting, Accounts Receivable was down USD 50,000 in the third quarter," credibility—and cooperation—can be challenged. If you cannot demonstrate it on paper, do not say it in the report. With respect to objectivity, adjectives and adverbs get report writers in trouble, so don't use them. Even the word *very* can have connotations that cause confusion. Stick with demonstrable facts. The IIA defines objectivity as "an unbiased mental attitude that allows internal auditors to perform engagements in such a manner that they have an honest belief in their work product and that no significant quality compromises are made."[5]

3. *Clarity* denotes lack of confusion and, in current parlance, transparency. Clarity means that everyone can see the implications of the conditions and findings. Clarity exists when it is transparently evident that not correcting high-level risk areas will have damaging effects not only on the bottom line but also on the company's

integrity. But the IIA didn't use the word *transparent*; it used the word *clear*, probably because it is clearer to more people. A cloud of confusion still hangs over the word *transparency*, probably because many people have used it inaccurately and nonobjectively. Word choice and sentence structure make writing clear; words are the subject of Chapter 6, and sentences of Chapter 7.

4. To many people, *concise* simply means being brief, but not so fast! Attempts to write concisely often leave out important details. Sometimes, to make the meaning clear, it is necessary to use more words. How to achieve conciseness is dealt with in detail in Chapter 6.

5. The word *constructive* implies something positive, with an eye toward a better future, toward improving the situation. As in constructive criticism, constructive recommendations are received more agreeably than comments about what *not* to do. *Constructive* means spelling out the benefits, not just the features. State exactly how the organization will save time or money when internal controls procedures are improved, rather than emphasizing the bells and whistles of the new system being recommended. Often, the most constructive writing begins in conversation. Discuss findings face-to-face, get reactions in person or on teleconference, and only commit the most constructive wording to the permanent record.

6. *Complete.* That's obvious, isn't it? When everything that needs to be said is said. But, just because 30 pages of words and tables have been generated does not mean the subject has been covered. What was it the audit committee asked to have clarified regarding reserves? Were all the manager's comments about control system deficiencies included? Are any pieces missing? Have someone else on your team review what you write. Only then can you be sure that your mind has not left something out. Pretend you are a programmer, because they don't skip steps! And reread what you have written at least once.

7. *Timely* is such a vague word, so it's a shame the IIA had to use it. But in this case, they would have had to substitute a whole laundry list of terms like quarterly, monthly, weekly, on demand—hey, that one has some zip! What the word *timely* means in most business contexts is, don't be late with the information—or it loses its power. Untimely reporting can mean the difference between happy shareholders, a satisfied CAE, and your promotion—and the untimely alternatives. Also be sure that the time frames for the data you are presenting are clearly established, make certain that end dates for recommendations are clearly stated, and delete any information that is out of date.

SOX Requirements

While the Sarbanes-Oxley Act of 2002 does not prescribe how traditional internal audit reports should be produced, the legislation has communication implications for those reports. Three sections are summarized here, Section 204: Auditor Reports to Audit Committees; Section 302: Corporate Responsibility for Financial Reports; and Section 404: Management Assessment of Internal Controls.

Section 204: Auditor Reports to Audit Committees

> The accounting firm must report to the audit committee all critical accounting policies and practices to be used, all alternative treatments of financial information within GAAP that have been discussed with management, ramifications of the use of such alternative disclosures and treatments, and the treatment preferred by the firm.[6]

Although this directive strictly applies only to public accounting firms, the fact that "alternative treatments of financial information" is mentioned suggests that internal auditors also take Section 204 into account, particularly because so much more communication is exchanged now among audit committees and internal auditors. The audit committee needs to be fully informed about any "ramifications of the use of such alternative disclosures and treatments," and the internal auditors can be the first to supply that information. Section 204 reminds auditors to notice any procedural changes and IT updates, analyze them, and be sure the committee is aware of them.

Section 302: Corporate Responsibility for Financial Reports

> The CEO and CFO of each issuer shall prepare a statement to accompany the audit report to certify the appropriateness of the financial statements and disclosures contained in the periodic report, and that those financial statements and disclosures fairly present, in all material respects, the operations and financial condition of the issuer.[7]

Again, the section is addressed to issuers of public company reports, but the essential concepts—appropriateness of financial statements and fair presentation of operations and financial condition—apply to the work of the internal audit function.

What is implied by reading between the lines of this standard is that reports had better be accessible—and concise—if top management is going to be able to certify their appropriateness.

Section 404: Management Assessment of Internal Controls

> Requires each annual report of an issuer to contain an internal control report which shall 1) state the responsibility of management for establishing and maintaining an adequate internal control structure and procedures for financial reporting; and 2) contain an assessment as of the end of the issuer's fiscal year, of the effectiveness of the internal control structure and procedures of the issuer for financial reporting. Each issuer shall attest to, and report on, the assessment made by the management of the issuer.[8]

Adequate internal controls and procedures for financial reporting have always been the domain of internal auditors; now, however, management must take responsibility and be fully informed about those controls and procedures so they can personally attest to them. This means that executives must be able to fully access all audit reports, which implies that the reports be structured and written so that readability and the motivation to act on the recommendations are high. In an ideal world: low risk probability and high readability!

SEC REGULATIONS

The Securities and Exchange Commission's domain is public companies and investors, but recent SEC rulings carry implications worth noting by internal auditors. In its rules to implement requirements of Section 404 of the Sarbanes-Oxley Act of 2002, the term "internal control over financial reporting" is defined to mean:

> A process designed by, or under the supervision of, the registrant's principal executive and principal financial officers, or person's performing similar functions, and effected by the registrant's board of directors, management and other personnel, to provide reasonable assurance regarding the reliability of financial reporting and the preparation of financial statements for external purposes in accordance with generally accepted accounting principles and includes those policies and procedures that
>
> - Pertain to the maintenance of records that in reasonable detail accurately and fairly reflect the transactions and dispositions of the assets of the registrant;
>
> - Provide reasonable assurance that the transactions are recorded as necessary to permit preparation of financial statements in accordance with generally accepted accounting principles, and receipts and expenditures of the registrant are being made only in accordance with authorizations of management and directors of the registrant; and
>
> - Provide reasonable assurance regarding prevention or timely detection of unauthorized acquisition, use or disposition of the registrant's assets that could have a material effect on the financial statements.[9]

From within that 165-word sentence (improved significantly by bullet points), the following concepts emerge and have relevance for internal audit report writing:

- Financial statement reliability
- Accurate records maintenance regarding company assets

- Transaction recording to permit preparation of financial statements
- Authorized receipts and expenditures only
- Prevention or timely detection of unauthorized use of assets

Internal auditors do not need to be told by the SEC what to include in their reports, but when such an influential organization hands down a checklist, it makes sense to use it.

PCAOB STANDARDS

As a private-sector, nonprofit corporation created by the Sarbanes-Oxley legislation, the PCAOB focuses on protecting investors and furthering the public interest in "the preparation of informative, fair and independent audit reports."[10] The PCAOB works closely with the SEC and is another agency that does not specifically govern the internal audit reporting process. However, the PCAOB has issued several standards regarding communication and monitoring that merit consideration. *Auditing Standard No. 2* deals with internal controls and is making a significant impact. Selections from AS2 are included in Appendix A of this book, but sections that have implications for process-driven reporting are described as follows:

> *Section 47.* The auditor should obtain an understanding of the design of specific controls by applying procedures that include:

- Making inquiries of appropriate management, supervisory, and staff personnel

- Inspecting company documents

- Observing the application of specific controls, and

- Tracing transactions through the information system relevant to financial reporting

> *Section 48.* The auditor could also apply additional procedures to obtain an understanding of the design of specific controls.[11]

Without quizzing the PCAOB about what they mean by "applying procedures" and applying "additional procedures," I would suggest that auditors use effective probes (meaning questions, not space vehicles) to get the information they need. Probes, which are explained in detail in Chapter 5, are invaluable communication tools for anyone in the information-gathering business. Asking the right questions is as important as having the right answers.

> *Section 207.* The auditor must communicate in writing to management and the audit committee all significant deficiencies and material weaknesses identified during the audit. The written communication should be made prior to the issuance of the auditor's report on internal control over financial reporting. The auditor's communication should distinguish clearly between those matters considered to be significant deficiencies and those considered to be material weaknesses, as defined in paragraphs 9 and 10 respectively.[12]

I will spare you having to flip to the Appendix and reprint the definitions here:

> A *significant deficiency* is a control deficiency, or combination of control deficiencies, that adversely affects the company's ability to initiate, authorize, record, process, or report external financial data reliably in accordance with generally accepted accounting principles such that there is more than a remote likelihood that a misstatement of the company's annual or interim financial statements that is more than inconsequential will not be prevented or detected.[13]

> A *material weakness* is defined as: a significant deficiency or combination of significant deficiencies, that results in more than a remote likelihood that a material misstatement of the annual or interim financial statements will not be prevented or detected.[14]

It is worth noting that both definitions focus on the company's ability to prevent or detect misstatements, rather than on monetary amounts to be exceeded. As for the complexity of the definitions and length of the sentences, I would suggest that qualifying phrases such as "annual" or "interim" be eliminated so that the essence of each definition can be more clearly understood. Both categories involve control deficiencies that affect a company's ability to guard against material misstatements in the financial statements.

With respect to communication tools and techniques, *Auditing Standard No. 3, Audit Documentation,* is also applicable to the internal audit process. Sections 4, 6, and 12 are particularly relevant.

For example, *Section 4* states:

> Also, the documentation should be appropriately organized to pro-
> vide a clear link to the significant findings or issues. Examples of
> audit documentation include memoranda, confirmations, corre-
> spondence, schedules, audit programs, and letters of representation.
> Audit documentation may be in the form of paper, electronic files,
> or other media.[15]

What is noteworthy about this section is its insistence on organization and linking, two of the seven key communication skills covered in
Chapter 1.

Section 6 makes another significant point: audit documentation should
be written in such a way that other professionals are able to comprehend
the full extent of the work, even if they were not present at the audit.

> Audit documentation must clearly demonstrate that the work was
> in fact performed. . . . Audit documentation must contain sufficient
> information to enable an experienced auditor having no previous
> connection with the engagement to understand the nature, timing,
> extent, and results of the procedures performed, evidence obtained,
> and conclusions reached; and to determine who performed the
> work and the date such work was completed, as well as the person
> who reviewed the work and the date of such review.[16]

This standard for clear and complete communication might be irrever-
ently referred to as the "what-if-the-writer-got-hit-by-a-truck?" scenario.
No matter how the cast of characters changes, audit documentation and
reports should remain accessible and comprehensible.

Section 12 deals with what is significant—and what is not.

> The auditor must document significant findings or issues, actions
> taken to address them (including additional evidence obtained), and
> the basis for the conclusions reached in connection with each engage-
> ment. Significant findings or issues are substantive matters that are
> important to the procedures performed, evidence obtained, or conclu-
> sions reached, and include, but are not limited to, the following:
>
> - Matters involving the selection, application, and consistency
>   of accounting principles, including related disclosures. Signif-
>   icant matters include, but are not limited to, accounting for
>   complex transactions, accounting estimates, and uncertain-
>   ties, as well as related management assumptions.

- Results of audit procedures that indicate a need for significant modification of planned auditing procedures, the existence of material misstatements, omissions in the financial statements, the existence of significant deficiencies, or material weaknesses in internal control over financial reporting.

- Audit adjustments, disagreements about final conclusions, circumstances that cause significant difficulty in applying auditing procedures, significant changes in the assessed level of audit risk, and any matters that could result in modification of the auditor's report.[17]

Finally, the frequently expressed desire of executives for "quality over quantity" reports is addressed in the *Appendix* to this particular PCAOB directive:

> The Board believes that the quality and integrity of an audit depends, in large part, on the existence of a complete and understandable record of the work the auditor performed, the conclusions the auditor reached, and the evidence the auditor obtained that supports those conclusions. . . . Clear and comprehensive audit documentation is essential to enhance the quality of the audit.[18]

Section A8 speaks directly to the value-adding characteristic of quality:

> The objective of this standard is to improve audit quality and enhance public confidence in the quality of auditing. Good audit documentation improves the quality of the work performed in many ways, including, for example:
>
> - Providing a record of actual work performed, which provides assurance that the auditor accomplishes the planned objectives
>
> - Facilitating the reviews performed by supervisors, managers, engagement partners, engagement quality reviewers, and PCAOB inspectors
>
> - Improving effectiveness and efficiency by reducing time-consuming, and sometimes inaccurate, oral explanation of what was done (or not done).[19]

AICPA PROFESSIONAL STANDARDS

Not all internal auditors are Certified Public Accountants; however, most accounting professionals consider AICPA professional standards in their practice.

SAS 112 probably has the greatest relevance for internal auditors and can be referenced at *http://www.aicpa.org/download/members/div/ auditstd/riasai/Recently_Issued_Standards_SAS_No_112.pdf.*

Report-related sections of the Standard specify that the written communication regarding significant deficiencies and material weaknesses identified during audits of financial statements, but not to express an opinion on the effectiveness of the entity's internal control over financial reporting. The Standard also specifies that the terms *significant deficiency* and, where relevant, *material weakness,* be defined.[20]

One possible way to express those components follows:

> The purpose of our audit of ABC Company as of December 31, 20XX, was to express an opinion on the financial statements, not on the effectiveness of ABC Company's internal controls. We conducted this audit in accordance with generally accepted auditing standards.
>
> One material weakness was identified: (insert description)
>
> (Insert *material weakness* definition, same as in PCAOB)
>
> The following significant deficiencies were identified:
>
> - (description)
> - (description)
> - (description)
>
> (Insert *significant deficiency* definition)

From an effective writing perspective, be sure to use parallel structure (see Chapter 6) on the bullet points, and check with the legal department before sending anything out.

REPLACEMENT FOR SAS NO. 61

As this book goes to press, the replacement for SAS No. 61 is being revised and also has relevance for internal auditors. The new standard, *The Auditor's Communication with Those Charged with Governance,* can be referenced at *http://www.aicpa.org/members/div/auditstd/ Proposed_Statement_of_Auditing_Standards.htm*

Key communication concepts to be aware of are maintaining two-way communication, determining appropriate people with whom to discuss particular matters, communicating significant findings in writing; and documenting all significant matters.

Adhering to these guidelines requires cooperation and communication between internal and external auditors and among internal auditors, CAEs, audit committees, and other financial managers and executives. Chapter 5 provides specific techniques to optimize the spoken communication these guidelines entail, and Chapters 6 through 9 describe how to make reports well-written—not rote.

THE COSO FRAMEWORK

The Committee of Sponsoring Organizations of the Treadway Commission (COSO) was formed in 1985 to identify the factors that cause fraudulent reporting and to make recommendations to reduce its occurrence. While some say this controls framework is outdated, a CFO magazine poll reported that 82 percent of respondents said they use the COSO framework for internal controls.[20]

COSO acknowledges the role that internal auditors play in evaluating the effectiveness of control systems:

> As an independent function reporting to the top management, Internal Audit is able to assess the internal control systems implemented by the organization and contribute to ongoing effectiveness. As such, Internal Audit often plays a significant monitoring role. In order to preserve its independence of judgment, Internal Audit should not take any direct responsibility in designing, establishing, or maintaining the controls it is supposed to evaluate. It may only advise on potential improvements to be made.[21]

The Executive Summary of the COSO framework is included in Appendix A. Here is one of the most relevant sections:

> **"Information and Communication**
>
> Pertinent information must be identified, captured and communicated in a form and timeframe that enable people to carry out their responsibilities. Information systems produce reports, containing

operational, financial and compliance-related information, that make it possible to run and control the business. They deal not only with internally generated data, but also information about external events, activities and conditions necessary to informed business decision-making and external reporting. Effective communication also must occur in a broader sense, flowing down, across and up the organization. All personnel must receive a clear message from top management that control responsibilities must be taken seriously. They must understand their own role in the internal control system, as well as how individual activities relate to the work of others. They must have a means of communicating significant information upstream. There also needs to be effective communication with external parties, such as customers, suppliers, regulators and shareholders."[22]

COMPANY STANDARDS

In addition to all the legal requirements, professional standards, and recommendations from regulatory bodies, many companies are adopting their own additional guidelines for internal audit reporting. These guidelines often include corporate style guides and listings of preferred word usages similar to those used by organizations such as the Associated Press.

Auditors new to public companies are encouraged to inquire about the existence of corporate style or report-writing guides. Auditors joining auditing firms or smaller companies should ask colleagues how titles are written and what should be capitalized, which preferred forms for currencies are used, and what report formats are in vogue. Asking is always better than assuming.

READABILITY STANDARDS

Last but not least, the standards for good writing should be followed. In the digital era, readable writing is decidedly less literary than it was when the classic *Harvard Business Review* article "What Do You Mean I Can't Write?" was written.[23] However, the basic elements that make written words readily understandable—and even interesting—remain constant, no matter what technology is used to put them on a page or screen.

The criteria for what to include in an audit vary depending on the type of audit, but the criteria for readability are the same, no matter what you write—from the shortest e-mail to the most complex report.

Here are the Rules for Readability:

1. *Focus on what the readers need to know.* Include only necessary information and connect the dots regarding findings and recommendations.
2. *Use appropriate, simple words.* Write to express, not impress.
3. *Link related ideas.* Keep subjects and verbs close together and put modifiers close to what they modify.
4. *Use billboards* (headings, subheadings, topic sentences) to let readers know what's coming. If they're not interested, they can move on.
5. *Get to the point.* Construct sentences and paragraphs to maximize meaning and minimize wordiness.
6. *Use punctuation, layout, and graphics to improve understanding.* Make the information look inviting.
7. *Be concise.* Do not be curt, but just use the right words to get the attention of people who are busy.
   (Section Three of this book contains specific tips and techniques on how to abide by the Rules for Readability.)

Note: The preceding review of SOX-inspired directives and traditional readability standards for internal audit reporting is by no means the last word. No matter what storms—or calms—prevail in the international business climate, best practices for communicating engagement results develop over time and are part of a continuing process. By working within that process, instead of holding to a fixed set of predetermined tasks, the chances for successful reporting increase exponentially.

Notes

1. Institute of Internal Auditors, "Internal Auditing's Role in Sections 302 and 404 of the U.S. Sarbanes-Oxley Act of 2002," Altamonte Springs, FL, May 26, 2004.
2. U. S. Sarbanes-Oxley Act of 2002, Section 404.
3. From *International Standards for the Professional Practice of Internal Auditing,* Introduction. Copyright 2004 by The Institute of Internal Auditors, Inc., 247 Maitland Avenue, Altamonte Springs, Florida 32710-4201 U.S.A. Reprinted with permission.
4. From *International Standards for the Professional Practice of Internal Auditing.* Copyright 2004 by The Institute of Internal Auditors, Inc., 247 Maitland Avenue, Altamonte Springs, Florida 32710-4201 U.S.A. Reprinted with permission.
5. Institute of Internal Auditors, *Standards,* Glossary.
6. AICPA, Summary of Sarbanes-Oxley Act of 2002, *www.aicpa .org/info/sarbanes_oxley_summary.htm.*
7. Ibid.
8. Ibid.
9. Securities and Exchange Commission, "SEC Implements Internal Control Provisions of Sarbanes-Oxley Act; Adopts Investment Company R&D Safe Harbor," Washington, D.C., May 27, 2003.
10. PCAOB, *www.pcaob.org.*
11. Public Company Accounting Oversight Board, Standards, AS2, Sections 47 and 48.
12. Ibid., Section 204.
13. Ibid., Section 9.
14. Ibid., Section 10.
15. Public Company Accounting Oversight Board, *Bylaws and Rules—Standards—AS3,* Section A4.
16. Ibid., Section A6.
17. Ibid., Section A12.
18. Public Company Accounting Oversight Board, *Bylaws and Rules—Standards—AS3,* Appendix A.
19. Public Company Accounting Oversight Board, Summary of Section 8.
20. Eric Laursen, "Automation and Sarbanes-Oxley Compliance," CFO.com, *www.cfo.com.*
21. COSO, *www.coso.org.*
22. COSO, Internal Control, Integrated Framework, Executive Summary, *www.coso.org/publications/executive_summary_integrated_ framework.htm.*
23. For more than 40 years, this article was the most requested reprint from the Harvard Business Press.

CHAPTER 3

NEW RULES AND NEW TOOLS

Perhaps even more than new rules, new tools are changing the way audit reports look and are produced. As the IIA revises the professional standards to clarify internal audit's role with respect to post-SOX reporting, software wizards are creating integrated and automated methods of collecting, reviewing, and storing data, and the audit process is being transformed. What was manual and detective is becoming automated and preventive.

According to an independent risk consulting firm:

> As companies simplify, standardize and automate their processes, they can expect greater emphasis on preventive controls (versus the detective controls that institutionalize costly and non-value added rework into processes) as well as increased emphasis on systems-based controls (versus the more costly, people-based controls). . . . As companies eliminate rework and build quality into their processes, they will reduce the number of manual journal entries required to close the books, streamline account reconciliation activity, deploy available configurable controls, and reduce the number of spreadsheets by transferring spreadsheet activity functionality into the organization's ERP system.[1]

From an IT standpoint, a major effect of SOX has been greater focus on protecting the integrity of corporate data. SOX compliance calls for identifying data that is subject to regulation, then defining data

management policies that, when followed, will fulfill the legal requirements regarding that data.[2] Therefore, because of the way data files are
captured and stored, and because of the increased demand for accurate,
fast transfer of information, IT is at the forefront of compliance efforts
in most companies, which has pluses and minuses for internal audit
reporting.

The advantages of using automated reporting software to comply
with new SOX-influenced standards and the communication challenges
of collaborating with IT professionals are the subjects of this chapter.

SAS THREE WAYS

SOX has made top-down, risk-based internal controls reporting a mandate and has inspired new Statements of Auditing Standards (SAS).
Statistical Analysis Systems (SAS) software, among others, has revolu-
tionized data capture, storage, and retrieval. And short attention spans
(SAS), combined with the new technologies, have generated an urgent
need for concise communication about risk assessment and the
adequacy of internal controls. (Remember this paragraph when we get
to the chapter on acronyms.) But even as the obvious advantages of
automation—speed and accuracy—are spelled out, the challenges that
accompany any new technological solution become apparent.

The SOX legislation has been a catalyst for automation, which, by its
nature, offers "repeatable, reliable, and predictable" solutions.[3] CFO
Research Services found that "automating the compliance and control
environment is a priority for 76 percent" of 180 companies surveyed,
and most executives think establishing a sustainable SOX compliance
framework will depend heavily on automation.[4] Traditional internal
audit reports will become more preventive and automated as well.

Whether the legislation remains fully in place is perhaps not as
significant as the positive effects it is having on creating an auditing
framework in which preventive steps can be taken, and in which
detective, after-the-fact attempts to fix things are no longer the best
practices.

But just how much knowledge of information technology do auditors need? The current IIA standard says:

> Internal auditors should have knowledge of key information technology risks and controls and available technology-based audit techniques to perform their assigned work. However, not all internal auditors are expected to have the expertise of an internal auditor whose primary responsibility is information technology auditing.[5]

Information about certifications and other IT auditor designations that are becoming more widespread can be found at the end of this chapter.

AUTOMATION ADVANTAGES

The most obvious advantages of automated reporting are speed and accuracy. In addition, management's desire for "just the main points" can be met with far less laborious cataloging—and far less likelihood of leaving something out. From a writing standpoint, the ability to automatically capture data and import it directly into the report document means that something will be there when that file is opened: no more blank-screen, empty-page trauma! Other advantages include the ability to leave comprehensive audit trails, auditor empowerment, preventive controls monitoring, and more robust data analysis.

Comprehensive Audit Trails

The creation of comprehensive audit trails is a documentation-related advantage of automated reporting. An audit committee member and accounting professor says: "Companies must . . . apply technology in an optimal manner which leaves comprehensive audit trails, thereby making it harder for documentation to be destroyed or fraud to be committed." She also says that because IT systems initiate, authorize, record, process, and report financial transactions, these systems all need to be assessed for SOX compliance.[6]

Auditor Empowerment

Having traceable, accurate information readily available is an advantage, particularly when internal auditors are working more with external auditors and audit committees. A software company CEO says IT empowers auditors in performing their traditional tasks:

> Business transactions are electronic footprints of business processes within an enterprise—and today's sophisticated IT environment comprises Enterprise Resource Planning (ERP) systems, as well as home-grown applications that facilitate business processes by automating those transactions and associated business workflows. For internal auditors, these automated systems give added confidence when they are facing the external auditors or audit committees because all the data for a particular period, instead of just a few random rows, can be accessed. These systems also test the data and display violations periodically instead of requiring that human resources be used for less reliable manual testing. This kind of continuous controls monitoring is one of the biggest advantages to having automated IT systems. And while auditors do not need to be experts in IT, the software methodologies and standards should be flexible enough to allow the auditors to perform their tasks effectively.[7]

Preventive Controls

Being able to look ahead to prevent problems, instead of only looking back to record them, is one of the biggest pluses offered by automated reporting. With respect to the preventive advantages of automation, a VP Corporate Controls of a major retailer said:

> During the internal controls gap analysis necessitated by Section 404, we recommended preventive system controls to close control gaps and then classified them as primary. This allowed us to both build efficiency into the process and reduce the time and cost necessary for testing; system controls testing does not require the large samples of manual data normally associated with manual controls. As an example, we identified restricted access to change inventory standard costs as a primary control governing our inventory valuation. Testing access requires very little time. And we rely on programming logic for the three-way match—a system control that automatically compares purchase order, invoice, and receiving date—as a primary control. As a result, we make a one-time test of

programming logic coupled with checking secure access to the program during our general computer controls testing.[8]

Robust Analysis

Because automated reporting gives auditors immediate access to more data, it can enhance their ability to analyze that data. One accounting firm partner notes that, with automation, the function performed by each individual will be more effective and efficient. "Automation adds value in that it permits a more robust analysis of the information that can result in identifying opportunities as well as risks or errors," he says.[9]

In the light of these advantages—and the need for speed and accuracy—businesses are turning more and more to automation technology. Consequently, internal auditors will have more interaction with technology and technologists, and therein lie many of the challenges.

AUTOMATION CHALLENGES

No matter how sophisticated the technology, the principle of garbage-in, garbage-out still applies. One of the automation obstacles is the misconception that automation automatically means accuracy. From a SOX perspective, it is critical to ensure the accuracy of any spreadsheets relied upon for financial reporting. Constant upgrading of technical skill is required to surmount the most obvious obstacle, which is the complexity of the systems.[10]

What these challenges mean for the internal audit reporting process is that the synthesis thinking and collaboration skills noted in Chapter 1 are becoming even more significant.

One international IT auditor recommends three things to be aware of, and she says they all revolve around the same theme: accounting and IT do not operate independently of each other; they are complementary to each other.

1. Systems are meant to make processes more efficient, not replace them. Just because a system has been implemented does not

guarantee that internal controls will function effectively. Controls need to be implemented within the system, and access to the controls (security features) should be reviewed.

2. When implementing a system, systems programmers and business units (e.g., finance, accounting) should maintain constant communication; otherwise, the system will not serve its purpose.

3. Although the implementation of automated controls may seem chaotic to operations in the early stages, such controls will, in the long run, streamline operations. How soon depends on the complexity of the controls and the operation's willingness to accept change.[11]

A VP and Chief Accountant says the key seems to be the filtering and organizing of information for management reviews, especially when working with large, data-intensive systems such as Oracle. He said:

> My experience has been with a monthly report produced by our IT group, which lists users who have accessed, processed, and possibly changed key information (like vendors in accounts payable). The first form of this report was next to impossible to review, given the volume of transactions passing through our Oracle accounting system. To make the material reviewable, our IT group put in some MS Excel pivot tables to show consolidated information on who did what, where in Oracle, and how many times they did it each month. These monthly reports are now easy to review and approve, and if I occasionally see a new name, I can track it down with the accounting group in India and find out who the new person is and whether they should be working in the area I am seeing on the report from IT.[12]

Security Issues

The issue of security is big. SOX requires significant controls over access to information and gives new emphasis to the tests for segregation of duties. To avoid the fox guarding the henhouse situation (i.e., asking the systems programmer for information they should not be accessing), basic open-ended probes should be made during the initial talk. What level of which operating system are we running? Who takes care of IT security (in general and platform-specific)?

Then there is the whole issue of physical security. "Better Secured IT Systems" are hailed in a discussion of dynamic audit processes and their outcomes by K.H. Spencer-Pickett:

> Many boards do not have a place for IT security on their agenda as they feel it is a technical matter. If there is no real security office in place, the auditors will need to make sure that the risk to corporate systems is properly understood and mitigated by management. Corporate governance has as a subset IT governance, through which business systems are protected and suitable contingency arrangements are made in the event of an attack, disaster, or systems failure.[13]

Speaking the Same Language

Creating a common platform of communication is vital. IT people think in a structured and disciplined manner (as do auditors) and rely heavily on flowcharts; therefore, it makes sense for auditors to use them when dealing with IT issues, and it also makes sense for internal auditors to get a definite idea of the IT architecture, hardware configurations, and various software applications associated with the business. Just being aware of which software details are associated with security, change control, and the audit trails will save hours of discussion, and possible altercation, later. Auditors can also benefit from using detailed questionnaires ahead of time and then working out further tweaks to the systems in person.

Every IT organization operates within its own culture, usually associated with specific key people (egos!), so questioning why policies exist, as opposed to how they work, will yield little positive benefit. Using a more consultative approach will create a more cooperative and effective atmosphere in which to do business. (For "consultative," read: "Frequent pauses to really hear what the other person is saying and frequent restatements of what has been said.")

Internal auditors need to be specific about the information they need and to ask questions about which particular methods are in place, without judging those methods. Editorial and subjective comments, such as: "That report is inadequate," should be avoided. Concentrate on specifics. For example: "That report contains three of the five items I need. How can I get the other two?"

WHAT WORKS AND WHAT DOES NOT?

Dealing with IT matters requires precise communication skills. Many internal auditors are fully updated on the technology, but many are not. Usually, talking with systems programmers to be sure the documentation handed over to the auditors matches up with the current software—and hardware—being used will solve the problem.

But, according to one mainframe systems programmer, the audit all too often works like this: The audit manager goes to the technology manager and announces there will be an audit. (There are no secret audits—those are called vulnerability and penetration tests, which are a piece of an audit.) Then the tech manager tells the audit manager that systems programmer so-and-so will supply the information. Ideally, this is known to all involved parties before the auditor shows up at the systems programmer's desk with the checklist. In any event, the checklist needs to be current for the system being audited.

FYI, presenting a checklist for an operating system version that hasn't been sold since the late 1990s (not that there aren't still some systems running it unsupported) will elicit the following reactions: (1) laughing out loud, (2) growling, or (3) the complete brush-off. It is critical to understand that many of the items on the checklist may be out of date and probably don't exist anymore—or function the same way.

Another scenario: Some auditors might ask for a SAS report on a particular subject when SAS software isn't even available on the system. And they might respond to that lack of software by asking the impossible: Well, when can you get it installed? This question is a Pandora's box of budgets, time, and ownership. If a report *must* be formatted by SAS, the auditors better be prepared to get out their checkbooks, because the techno-manager is going to tell the audit-manager that he or she gets to pay for the install.

A more effective approach is to ask for what is needed in a readable format. If the shop doesn't currently have a way of formatting the data into a readable, usable format, it doesn't mean the data is not there; it just means it isn't immediately available for a report, and it may mean that the techno-manager will have to budget some time for the systems programmer to create such a report.

In terms of effective communication, viable requests need to be made—back to the validity of that checklist—and confirmation that the information being sought is still generated must be secured.

Note: Anyone working with an IBM mainframe should get a copy of the System Management Facility (SMF) reference guide (free from the IBM Web site *www-03.ibm.com/servers/eserver/zseries/zos/*), which shows every available record type on an IBM mainframe and contains pertinent information about any system. Make sure the requested files (1) still exist and (2) still contain the same information. Then review these (assuming the checklist is old) for new record types and subtypes that would be helpful for an audit. Most operating systems on most platforms have something similar to record the events on their respective systems.[14]

PERSPECTIVE

Systems Programmer B.L. Jeffery says miscommunication between auditors and IT personnel is the cause of many preventable problems. She advises: "Beware of those checklists; some are current, many are not. Sit down with the systems programmer before you start, and get the latest word." And she has positive comments about mainframes: "They're still the biggest and fastest and most stable framework for many large companies to manage; mainframes have been doing things for years that other operating systems are just developing—multiprocessing, data storage techniques, tight security—have you ever heard of a virus infecting an IBM MVS operating system? Urban legends hint there may have been a couple, but I couldn't find any concrete evidence."

WHAT REALLY DOES NOT WORK?

At the top of any communication *faux pas* list is the end run. When some auditors do not get the information they need, or think they need, from the person assigned to help them, or they think the answer isn't correct, they just query other systems programmers for a better answer! Playing people off against each other is not a professional or productive way to do business. Not every IT professional is totally up-to-date either; if the auditors know the answer is incorrect, they should just say so and produce documentation to back up their answer. Then, if the systems programmer gets upset, they should take the issue to the techno-manager.[15]

Note: As this very large array of new technologies continues to expand, the need for more specialized technical knowledge by internal auditors will continue to grow as well. Demand and appreciation for the Certified Information Systems Auditor (CISA) designation is becoming more widespread. Two major business groups in India now recognize it: (1) the National Stock Exchange sees CISA as integral to its system auditing guidelines; and (2) the Computer Emergency Response Team India (CERT-In) is keen on security auditors who possess the designation.

IT TIPS AND TECHNIQUES

Five questions to ask yourself—or the systems programmer—before beginning an IT audit:

1. Do I understand the platform being audited (e.g., mainframe, midrange, Windows-based, UNIX/AIX, Linux, Unisys, HP) hardware and software?
2. What level of which operating system is being run?
3. Who takes care of IT security?
4. Is adequate software licensed and installed on the platform to generate, in a readable format, the information I need?
5. If the answers I get are not adequate or correct, who should I go to?

Notes

1. PCAOB/SEC Roundtable, May 10, 2006. Comments by James W. DeLoach, Jr., Protiviti, *www.sec.gov/news/press/4-511.shtml.*
2. Jon William Toigo, "IT Sense," *z/Journal*, February/March, 2005.
3. Eric Laursen, "Automation and Sarbanes-Oxley Compliance," CFO.com, October 18, 2005.
4. Ibid.
5. From *Standards* 1210.A3. Copyright 2004 by The Institute of Internal Auditors, Inc., 247 Maitland Avenue, Altamonte Springs, Florida 32710-4201 U.S.A. Reprinted with permission.
6. Ann Brooks, Audit Committee member and University of New Mexico Accounting Professor, e-mail correspondence, April 2006.
7. Anand Adya, President and CEO, Greenlight Technologies, e-mail correspondence, June 2006.
8. Joe Nici, VP Corporate Controls, The MOVADO Group, e-mail correspondence, June 2006.
9. Steve Newstead, Partner, RubinBrown, e-mail correspondence, April 2006.
10. Ibid.
11. Shirley Nguyen, IT auditor, Schlumberger Ltd., e-mail correspondence, May 2006.
12. Bruce Fortelka, Vice President and Chief Accountant, Kanbay, e-mail correspondence, June 2006.
13. K.H. Spencer Pickett, *Audit Planning: A Risk-Based Approach* (Hoboken, NJ: John Wiley & Sons, 2006).
14. B.L. Jeffery, Systems Programmer, e-mail correspondence, June 2006.
15. Ibid.

GOING WITH
THE FLOW

The only important distinction is between good writing and bad writing. Good writing is good writing, whatever form it takes and whatever we call it.

William Zinsser, *On Writing Well*

The form audit reports take is changing. Long narratives are out, tables and dashboards that condense complex data are in, and fully automated reports are coming on strong. The act of writing—by which we mean ordering words and symbols and inscribing them somewhere in such a way that a message is conveyed—is still required. But written reports look dramatically different than they did in the old days—a year ago!

Chapter 4 offers examples of templates and a hot-off-the-computer format for producing internal audit reports. But many formats are possible and, as the demand for compact, easily accessible, and attestable reports increases, internal auditors, managers, CAEs, and audit committees need to pool their collective wisdom and agree on the most practical technological tools to use. Formatting is not necessarily a one-size-fits-all operation, and any template should be tailored to specific needs. "Process-driven" means open to circumstances as they occur.

As the physical appearance of reports is altered, effective spoken communication throughout the audit process takes on greater importance. Assuming that everyone will notice what is significant in a new format and respond accordingly is not a good idea; discussing what works, what doesn't, and what's different is important. Therefore, Chapter 5 offers ways to get the most out of the spoken word—a too-often-overlooked component of every report. Tips on how to ask effectively for what you want and elicit maximum cooperation are also presented.

CHAPTER 4

NEW LOOKS FOR AUDIT REPORTS

Information visualization is the key to creating knowledge from data. However, as data sets become larger and more complex, the capability to visualize and effectively package them often lags behind the ability to collect the raw material.

Internal auditors routinely examine enormous volumes of data, and the stakes are higher, since SOX, for omissions or misstatements. In attempting to include every material control deficiency and potential risk, how can dreaded data dumps—and the response of TMI—be avoided? If too much information is provided, report writers run the risks of losing readers and losing focus.

Presenting quantitative information in an appealing format is more than just cosmetic nicety; clean layouts contribute to comprehension and clarity of message. Also, it is easier to pay attention to—and care about—information that is attractively presented, especially when it is complex.

ADVANTAGES OF AUTOMATED, LIMITED SPACE

Fortunately, tabular reports and automated formats have arrived. Verbiage that is literally boxed and packaged is now being used, even in the Executive Summaries of many internal audit reports. Longer, more literary phrasings are being replaced by words that are better suited to defined-format space—and short attention spans.

However, highly condensed, telegraphic-style writing can be difficult to decipher, particularly when the subject matter is technical and filled with acronyms (what *does* SAS stand for?),[1] symbols (such as dollar signs and decimals), and code words (quick, define the term "data governance"). Modular report formats, such as the tables generated by MS Excel, are beneficial only when the information they contain is not only complete but also easy to understand.

The whole point of filling a set of boxes with information is to provide an instantly comprehensible snapshot of salient points, while maintaining the connections between those points. Demonstrating the relationships among discrete items has always been a key element in effective audit reporting, and SOX has made that kind of effectiveness a legal requirement.

In addition to placing related chunks of information in proximity on a page, tabular formats have another significant advantage over traditional text: they provide a prescribed space to be filled. Because tables offer definite enclosures in which to present related numbers or narrative, they force report writers to make more disciplined decisions about what to include. Having a limited area to fill is actually helpful, and when text is enclosed within an MS Excel cell, the relationships among the various words and sentences are automatically assumed by the reader.

Furthermore, using reporting software that automatically imports text from other files imposes a word-choice discipline on the writer and discourages rambling—not to mention eliminating the trauma of having to face the blank page or screen!

Poets have long recognized the message-reinforcement value of using word patterns and rhythms, such as iambic pentameter. The current popularity of "fibs"—haiku-like poems based on the Fibonacci sequence, with one syllable in the first line, then two, then three, then five, and so on—attests to the continuing appeal of word patterns. With respect to fibs, a screenwriter and film production assistant said: "How great that something mathematical could be bringing together all sorts of people who don't write professionally and giving them a form."[2] Internal auditors have shared such a form for years.

CLEAR EXPECTATIONS AND COMPANY EXPECTATIONS

Predefined formats establish clear expectations for readers. Magazines and newspapers, even Web sites, position their regular departments in approximately the same place in each issue or iteration because readers expect them to be there—and respond accordingly.

In most internal audit reports, expectations are established, and reinforced, by the Table of Contents (TOC). Many reports include a cover letter followed by a TOC, which typically lists such items as the Executive Summary, specific objectives or areas of concentration, and conclusions or recommendations. Backup documentation, for those who require greater detail, can be included in appendices. In fact, appendices were probably the first place tabular formats and MS Excel were widely used.

In terms of traditional report formats, most companies provide a corporate style guide that specifies graphics and spacing, fonts and sizes, and rules for capitalization. Some of the topics covered in a typical style guide are phrases to use or avoid, words to capitalize, how to show titles and geographic segments, in what order to list audit components, and how to express international currencies. Ask whether your company has a style guide; internal auditors in my seminars have often been surprised to find out that such an item existed.

In terms of SOX report formats and emerging software-generated formats, the guidelines are being drawn up as this book is being written. The IIA conference, held in Florida the week of June 19, 2006, undoubtedly included discussions about how best to package the information needed by audit committees and required by SOX.

Meanwhile, five basic principles for any effective format are:

1. First things first. Position the most important information upfront, on top.
2. Keep fonts simple, and do not mix them. Choose a clean font and stick with it.
3. Do not overemphasize. Use caps, underlines, italics, and boldface sparingly.
4. Be generous with white space; and don't cram too much data into a small area.
5. Use headings and terms that people understand.

SAMPLE TEMPLATES

The following report templates illustrate three different ways of organizing audit report information. Regardless of what kind of audit is being reported, the categories should be in accordance with the IIA's International Standards for the Professional Practice of Internal Auditing.

The first template, Exhibit 4.1, applies to an internal audit, and the primary components are Project Overview and Scope, Executive Summary, and Opportunities for Improvement.[3]

The second template, Exhibit 4.2, applies to a financial institution audit and includes Overview, Audit Findings and Recommendations, and Summary of Internal Audit Scope and Staffing. An Executive Summary may also be included depending on the length and complexity of the report.[4]

The third template, Exhibit 4.3, is used for an IT Management Deficiency Report. Key components are controls that failed, management's response, and the action plan and target date for completion.[5] As the internal auditing process becomes more automated, templates such as these can be expected to be more widely used.

EXHIBIT **4.1** *Internal Audit Report Template*

CLIENT NAME

PROJECT NAME
DATE

EXHIBIT 4.1   *(continued)*

Date

XX
CLIENT NAME
XX (typically addressed to the CFO or the Chair of the Audit Committee)
XX

Re: Review of PROJECT NAME

Dear XX:

In conjunction with our overall engagement to provide internal audit services to CLIENT NAME, we have completed our review of PROJECT NAME. Our services were performed in accordance with the applicable Standards for the Professional Practice of Internal Auditing as prescribed by the Institute of Internal Auditors.

This report is being provided without management comments, which should be provided to YY within 30 days.

The accompanying report includes a Project Overview, Executive Summary, and Opportunities for Improvement. Because the procedures performed in conjunction with the assessment are more limited than those required to provide an opinion on the system of internal accounting control as a whole, such an opinion is not expressed. In addition, the engagement did not include a detailed audit of transactions required to discover fraud, defalcations, or other irregularities.

This report is intended solely for the information and use of management and is not intended to be, and should not be, used by anyone other than these specified parties. CLIENT NAME's external auditors and regulators may be provided with a copy of this report in connection with fulfilling their respective responsibilities.

We would like to express our gratitude to all employees involved with this project. Each person involved was accessible and responsive to our requests for information.

Sincerely,

AUDIT FIRM NAME

Signature information

cc: YY

EXHIBIT **4.1**   *(continued)*

CLIENT NAME
PROJECT NAME
Date

Table of Contents

	Page
Project Overview	1
Executive Summary	x
Opportunities for Improvement	x

EXHIBIT 4.1   *(continued)*

<u>Project Overview</u>

We have completed a review of PROJECT NAME.

The objectives of our review were to:

- Determine whether . . .

Note: Objectives of the review are decided jointly by the client and internal auditors in the audit planning meetings. The Project Overview section varies in length depending on the number of specific objectives. Each objective is stated as concisely and specifically as possible and, using parallel structure, begins with an action to be performed.

EXHIBIT 4.1 *(continued)*

<u>Executive Summary</u>

Internal controls over . . .

(Areas under review are ranked: adequate, need improvement, not adequate.)

Note: Standard paragraph format is used in the Executive Summary, with tables if needed. The Summary has no specified length limitation but depends on the number of objectives previously stated—the shorter, the better.

The objective is to summarize on one page the key findings/issues in the body of the report.

EXHIBIT 4.2   *Financial Institution Audit Report Template*

INTERNAL AUDIT REPORT

(Audit Area)
(Report Date)
(As of Date)
(Report #)

Note: Every cover page, in addition to specifying the audit content, should always contain the proper dates. And in the draft step of the writing process, each version should be dated!

EXHIBIT **4.2** *(continued)*

(Audit Area)
(Report Date)
(As of Date)
(Report #)

CONTENTS

I. Overview 1

II. Audit Findings and Recommendations ....

III. Summary of Internal Audit Scope and Staffing ....

Exhibit 4.2   *(continued)*

I. Overview

The (name of bank department) is located in (city, state) in the (e.g., Business Operations Center). The area is responsible for processing, verifying, and executing (e.g., incoming and outgoing wire transfers).

The area processes (types of transactions: e.g., domestic wire transfers through the Federal Reserve Bank using the Fedline system; international wire transfer requests are processed through XXX with the activity being settled via a daily wire transfer).

(Name of auditing firm) performed an audit of the (audit area) function of (name of Bank) (the Corporation) as of (audit date). Our work focused on certain of the Bank's policies and procedures in these areas, based on an assessment by your management, with which we concurred, that the overall risk for these areas was (high, moderate, or low). Our work was completed in compliance with the Standards of The Institute of Internal Auditors.

(If multiple areas):

Our work focused on certain of the Bank's policies and procedures in these areas, based on an assessment by your management, with which we concurred, that the overall risk for these areas was as follows:

Area	Management's Risk Assessment

As we discussed with management and with the Audit Committee at the (date) meeting, we disagree with management's assessment of risk in the following areas:

Area	Management's Risk Assessment	Audit Firm's Risk Suggestion

EXHIBIT 4.2 *(continued)*

Your Audit Coordinator approved our work plan, based on this risk assessment, and we communicated the work we did and our results to management and your Audit Coordinator. The overall objective of the audit was to review the controls over the (audit area/s). We reviewed selected policies and procedures, discussed compliance with these policies and procedures with Bank personnel, and tested certain detail records. In this report, we provide a summary of our findings and recommendations along with management's responses.

To assist you in analyzing our recommendations, we have provided our suggestions for corrective action, based on the finding's exposure to loss, as follows:

> ***High:*** Represents an issue requiring immediate remedy by management and which, if left uncorrected, exposes the Bank to risk of loss or misappropriation of assets or to increased regulatory scrutiny.

> ***Moderate:*** Represents an issue requiring timely remedy by management and which, if left uncorrected, may expose the Bank to risk of loss or misappropriation of bank assets. Periodic training should include these issues.

> ***Low:*** Represents an issue for consideration by management for correction or implementation. Low-risk areas are not considered to represent significant or immediate risk to the Bank. However, repeated oversights without corrective action or compensating controls could lead to increased regulatory scrutiny. Discussions with personnel and/or additional training regarding these issues would be beneficial.

> ***Best Practice:*** Represents an issue for consideration by management for correction or implementation based on best practices noted in the industry.

Section 404 Compliance Testing

Additionally, we have identified any findings or recommendations that are also related to Sarbanes-Oxley Section 404 testing of controls identified by management as "key controls."

EXHIBIT 4.2   *(continued)*

II. **Audit Findings and Recommendations**

Finding #: (Title)

Risk Rating: (High, Moderate, Low, Best Practice)

This comment also relates to testing completed on the following Sarbanes-Oxley Section 404 key control defined by management:

Description (includes the effects of the observed condition or situation)

Implication (what matters about this condition)

Recommendation (what can be done to improve the situation)

Management's Action Plan (management's response and what they will do)

Individual(s) Responsible: (commitment by specific individuals)

Due Date: (by when)

EXHIBIT 4.2 *(continued)*

III. Summary of Internal Audit Scope and Staffing

The scope of the internal audit included testing in the following activities and processes:

- (brief descriptions of specific conditions or situations)
-
-

The specific procedures performed related to the internal audit were based on the concepts of selective testing. Although our testing was performed in some areas without exception, we can provide no assurance that exceptions would not have been detected had procedures been changed or expanded.

It should also be recognized that internal controls are designed to provide reasonable, but not absolute, assurance that errors and irregularities will not occur, and that procedures are performed in accordance with management's intentions.

There are inherent limitations that should be recognized in considering the potential effectiveness of any system of internal controls. In the performance of most control procedures, errors can result from misunderstanding of instructions, mistakes in judgment, carelessness, or other personal factors. Internal control procedures can be circumvented intentionally by management with respect to the execution and recording of transactions, or with respect to the estimates and judgments required in the processing of data. Further, the projection of any evaluation of internal control to future periods is subject to the risk that the procedures may become inadequate because of changes in conditions, and that the degree of compliance with procedures may deteriorate.

EXHIBIT 4.3 *IT Management Deficiency Report Template*

The term "Sub-Cycle" describes which of five domains the report covers, such as change management or security; "Phase" refers to either a Test of Efficiency (TOE) or a Test of Design (TOD).

IT Management Deficiency Report

date

Sub-Cycle:		
Phase:	TOD/TOE	

Gap # WT/T Ref. #	Source	Date Reported	Sub-cycle	Key Control Ref #	Description of Issue/Exception	Issue Type (A)
Test of Design Deficiencies						
Test of Effectiveness Deficiencies						

Legend

A | Issue Type - Design Effectiveness, Operating Effectiveness, Documentation Issue, Recommendation/Enhancement

B | Status - Open, Closed

72

EXHIBIT 4.3 *(continued)*

Control Process/ Documentation Requires Revision Y/N	Control Owner	Management Response (Action Plan)	Status (B)	Action Plan Target Completion Date	Action Plan Revised Completion Date	Action Plan Date Completed	Results of Remediation Testing Pass / Fail	Comments

ORGANIZATIONAL METHODS

No matter which format is used, the basic principles of organization should be followed. In narrative formats, start with the most important information and work back to include supporting data and information of lesser significance

Stating the most material conclusions first is the *order of importance* method of organization and is most practical when busy executives are likely to stop reading to take an urgent phone call or leave the audit meeting before the presentation is completed.

Many other organizational methods exist; and three that may be particularly useful in an audit or financial management report are:

1. *Functional,* which describes conditions department by department. This method is valuable for preacquisition evaluations and other operations reporting.
2. *Comparative,* which presents advantages and disadvantages or strengths and weaknesses of two or more situations. Comparisons may be called for when reporting on specific time frames or on different company locations.
3. *Analytical,* which examines a situation by breaking it down into parts and explaining the implications of each. This kind of analysis may become part of an otherwise "order of importance" report when the subject is complex.

Using preset or tabular formats simplifies the "how to organize" decision. Many companies use established headings and subheadings that can simplify the organizational step in the audit report process. When tabular formats are used, the highest priority items should be given the greatest graphic emphasis.

FORMAT TOOLS AND TECHNIQUES

Tables and appendices do the heavy lifting with respect to detailed data. By clearing the executive summary and body of the report of extraneous narrative, internal auditors are able to focus attention on the big picture—the one the audit committee and managers need to see. Specific Tips and Techniques for incorporating formal graphic elements, such as tables and graphs, are provided in Chapter 9.

Headings and subheadings, paragraph breaks, and appropriate spacing also make it easier for executives to focus on the main points and see clearly what actions should be taken. Judicious use of white space to create a frame for significant information effectively focuses readers on what matters most. Any automated formats should be designed accordingly.

Announcing what is coming is another technique that works like a charm. If readers are interested in what is announced, they continue; if not, they can quickly move on. Setting up a system of billboards made up of headings and subheadings also helps writers because they can quickly check whether the subjects they intended to include have made the cut.

A word on automated style: Not too long ago, formal language was the norm in most financial reports. Internal auditors who are romance-language natives still feel more comfortable with lengthier sentences and more stylistically flowing prose. Business English, however, is simply not the place for elegant writing; it is the place for efficient writing.

Automated formats are effective tools for conveying quantitative information, but the message is what matters. The internal auditor determines what that message should be.

Notes

1. Chapter 3 of this book, page 44.
2. Emily Galvin, a screenwriter and film production assistant, wrote one of her plays using the Fibonacci sequence but used it to regulate the number of words in each line instead of the number of syllables. *http://timesofindia.indiatimes.com/articleshow/1491761.cms*
3. Courtesy of RubinBrown, St. Louis, MO.
4. Courtesy of Crowe Chizek and Company LLC, Oakbrook, IL.
5. Courtesy of DIONEX Corp., Sunnyvale, CA.

CHAPTER 5

THE VALUE-ADDED SPOKEN (AND E-MAILED) WORD

A s audits become automated—and inundated by new regulations—internal auditors work at a congested intersection of tools and content. At such a juncture, teamwork and oral communication take on new importance. Cutting-edge techno-tools often yield unanticipated results, and the consequent learning curves can be shortened through effective conversation. The clarification of new standards, as discussed in Chapter 2, is also accelerated by healthy discussion.

When people are just starting to use new, unfamiliar methodologies to accomplish old, familiar tasks, workplace conversations can actually add value rather than waste time. When the first desktop computers arrived at KPMG, for instance, everybody gathered in the partner offices that had one and taught each other how to get the most out of the new equipment—and that was after the formal training sessions. In the post-SOX era, collaborative discussions about how the new controls software functions in real time or where repetitive testing might be eliminated will also add value to the enterprise.

This chapter outlines several techniques to make optimum use of all the chitchat—from water cooler conversations to cell phone conferences to impromptu meetings in hallways or aboard transoceanic flights. Tips on how to ask the right questions and say the right things during walkthroughs are also included, and e-mail etiquette is covered too.

SHARED INTERPRETATIONS ARE VALUABLE

Without the opportunity to share ideas and trade insights, most businesspeople quickly lose their connection with what is really going on, and, as the following anecdote illustrates, risk losing valuable information.

In a story about a study at Xerox PARC, the authors of *The Social Life of Information* salute the value of OJT—on-the-job talking. The Xerox reps, whose job was to fix any machine that broke down, were given manuals that explained what to do in specific circumstances, but the manuals did not provide sufficient information to fix things that weren't on the menu or explain why certain things should be done. Therefore, the reps more often relied on each other—and on the war stories they told each other about what worked and what didn't—to get many of the machines fixed.[1]

Any truly workable and sustainable process that involves people includes open-ended elements such as collaboration, narration, and improvisation. These vital elements require experience sharing, conversation, and dialogue—that is, spoken words. By discussing what they observe and experience, auditors expand their understanding of the "why" behind certain tests and standards and, in the process, can get to the source of problems more efficiently.

What constitutes this collective wisdom is not just shared stories or shared information, but also shared interpretations. These interpretations comprise the knowledge base that binds people and companies together, and sharing them constitutes the most productive type of workplace communication.

IIA RECOMMENDATIONS

With its insistence on accountability and closer controls monitoring, SOX has actually generated a need for more of this kind of productive communication regarding audit results.

The "Recommended Role of Internal Audit," as described by the IIA, specifies that internal audit's support for management include the following activities, most of which require spoken communication skills:

- Providing advice and recommendations
- Acting as facilitator between the external auditor and management
- Providing internal audit documentation for processes under scope
- Advising on best practices
- Aiding in identifying control gaps and reviewing management plans for correcting control gaps
- Acting as coordinator between management and the external auditor regarding scope and plans for testing[2]

All of these tasks will most likely involve some e-mail as well, and all will definitely require keen listening skills.

The most charismatic speakers are usually superb listeners. For example, Betty Friedan, Jerry Falwell, Richard Lamm, and William Kunstler were about to participate in "Last Words," a special video presentation being taped at Denver's Trinity Church. At an International Women's Forum meeting preceding the taping, a group of us met with Ms. Friedan, but, rather than try to impress us with what she had to say, she asked questions and listened to our answers. Later, when the diminutive speaker ascended to the podium, she fired up the room with remarks that were enlivened by the information she had collected. After practicing careful observation and synthesis thinking, she presented her findings in a most compelling manner.

Chapter 1 offered Listening Tips and Techniques in the context of the audit process, and Chapter 10 will cover international listening considerations, but when it comes to communicating effectively when conversing, the "two ears, one mouth" ratio is the main thing to concentrate on.

A post-SOX article promoted by the AICPA says that: "In addition to beefing up the department's financial expertise, new internal auditors are being asked to expand their interpersonal skills."[3] Indeed. Enough said.

GENERAL COMMUNICATION TIPS AND TECHNIQUES

1. How to value and interpret data matters more than reciting a laundry list of factoids. We are valued for how we think, not what we know.
2. Visual words that create pictures in the minds of the readers or audience are more effective than abstract terms.
3. Know that audiences and readers are asking themselves three questions:
   - Do I want to listen to or read this?
   - Do I believe this?
   - How will this affect me?
4. Be compelling rather than right.
5. Make it short—and personal.
6. Make problems yours as well as theirs.
7. Say: "You're right" instead of "I know."
8. Deal with present issues, not problems from the past.
9. Avoid using the phrases always, never, no one ever, everyone always.
10. Underpromise and overperform.

SPEAK BEFORE YOU WRITE

Using spoken words to communicate during the process of writing an internal audit report has always made good sense. Once words are recorded—on paper, on hard drive, in cyberspace—they take on added weight and may come across with more power than the writer intends. And printed words are difficult to retract. Therefore, refrain from ever writing anything you may not want to see reprinted somewhere later. Contentious control issues that can be clarified ahead of time in conversation also become easier to incorporate into the report and much easier to agree to in the follow-up review.

Honest, open dialogue without attachment to specific outcomes can also prevent long-winded, nonproductive arguments and pave the way for progress.

ASK THE RIGHT QUESTIONS

By asking more questions upfront—and taking notes on the conversations as well as the internal control information—auditors can get a much clearer idea of what is expected, the situation being reported, and the optimum recommendations.

Professional writers would not think of submitting articles for publication without discussions with the editors, yet auditors sometimes seem to think they are expected to know what management's concerns are without asking. After perhaps only one audit planning meeting, in which managers assume they have explained their expectations, the internal auditors assume they know what to do, and the stage is set for a series of extraneous meetings, phone calls, and e-mails that might have been avoided.

Probing for information does not need to be an intrusion. Like most interactions between people, it all depends on how the words are used and the questions are asked. After all, whether it's an instrumented spacecraft or a series of specific questions, a "probe" is nothing more than a method of discovering information.

THE IMPORTANCE OF PROBES

Robert E. Lefton, Ph.D., believes probing is the single most important communication skill for internal auditors because they are in the information-gathering business.[4] He cites eight different kinds of probes, from open-end probes and pauses, which encourage the other person to open up and keep talking, to leading questions and summary statements, which help confirm what has been said. Too many closed-end questions ("Are the Receivables files complete?") or brief assertions ("I see. Okay.") do not give respondents much room to expand on the subject and therefore do not deliver much information. Open-end probes ("What was your take on that meeting?") pull other people into the subject matter by inviting them to comment, and the conversation can go further and into greater detail. "At least 15 to 25 seconds should elapse before you break the silence after making an open-end probe," says Lefton. "Give the respondent time to think, because after those pauses is when you get the gold: information you never imagined you would get."[5]

Probing also increases receptivity, and when someone asks a question back, you know they have bought into the subject and are invested in the outcome. It is no longer you against them. And, Lefton says, like any other skill, effective probes can be learned through practice.[6]

However, if IT professionals or operations people being audited hear the questions as unreasonable demands rather than valid requests, they are less likely to cooperate. And if the auditors are unclear about what they are asking—and why—respondents will be unable to cooperate and justifiably annoyed.

"What if?" questions can lead to productive discussion, especially in the planning stages of an IT audit. Two other powerful, open-ended probes are: "What do you want?" and "What are you getting that you don't want?"

The right questions reinforce the whole process. Sometimes data-limiting inquiries (as opposed to "tell me all you know") are easier for reluctant (and swamped) respondents to deal with. Ask "What three items on this punch list are most important?" Not "What are the biggest problems in setting up the new system?" And sometimes volunteering unconfirmed information such as "Weren't the Accounts Payable listings off by 30 percent?" motivates the respondent to correct you, and is an effective way to get feedback.

The PCAOB recognizes the value of inquiry. *Section 81 of AS2* says:

> To corroborate information at various points in the walkthrough, the auditor might ask personnel to describe their understanding of the previous and succeeding processing or control activities and to demonstrate what they do. In addition, inquiries should include follow-up questions that could help identify the abuse of controls or indicators of fraud.

Examples of follow-up inquiries include asking personnel:

> What they do when they find an error or what they are looking for to determine if there is an error (rather than simply asking them if they perform listed procedures and controls); what kind of errors they have found; what happened as a result of finding the errors, and how the errors were resolved. If the person being interviewed has never found an error, the auditor should evaluate whether that is because of good preventive controls or whether the individual performing the control lacks the necessary skills.

> Whether they have ever been asked to override the process or controls, and if so, to describe the situation, why it occurred, and what happened.[7]

An entire chapter could be written on the best way to communicate while conducting walkthroughs; but the primary communication techniques to use are objective, fact-based, nonaccusatory words—combined with mutual respect.

THE POWER OF PROGRAMMING AND DEFERENCE

Even potentially combative conversations can be productive if they are set up to succeed. It's possible to program for positive outcomes by stating what you want, not what you don't want. For instance "Let's look at this system and determine the three primary deficiencies." Not "This system is out of whack, and it's going to take a long time to figure out what's wrong."

Positive probing (asking specific questions) also helps keep adversarial discussions on track, but occasionally, even the most carefully worded statement or question can expose unexpected tension. In such a situation, particularly if the other person is in a politically superior position, confident deference is the skill to use.

To confidently defer means to yield, for the moment, with courtesy, to give in to the wish of another, as in showing respect. Deferring on a point of disagreement is not an agreement or a giving up, but a strategic action that leaves an opening for further discussion.

Marshall Rosenberg, Founder and Educational Director of the Center for Nonviolent Communication (*www.cnvc.org*), offers many practical suggestions about how to use spoken words effectively. Here are five:

1. Instead of saying what you *don't* want someone to do, say what you *do* want the person to do.
2. Instead of saying what you want someone to *be*, such as "more prompt," say what action you would like the person to take.
3. Take a minute each day to think about how you would like to relate to yourself and others. What are you after?
4. Check your intention to see if you are as interested in others getting their needs met as in meeting your own.
5. When asking someone to do something, check first to see if you are making a request or a demand.[8]

TELEPHONE TALK

The telephone, despite its ubiquity thanks to cellular and satellite technology, is not a perfect medium of communication. We still cannot adequately see who we are talking to. Body movements are not conveyed, so we cannot perceive the sagging shoulders, wicked grins, rolling eyes, or bored facial expressions, and the person on the other end cannot see ours. Tonal quality and vocal inflections on the phone are more expressive than those dry e-mails, but the telephone still hides a multitude of meanings.

How to use it most effectively? For openers, market research firms train telemarketers to smile as they speak and imagine the person on the other end as someone unique, not as simply a name to be checked off a list.

Effective telephone communication should exhibit the same principles of organization and specificity as written words, plus one more: empower your voice! "This is Jane Smith, I would like to speak with Mr. Audit Committee Chair." By identifying yourself with confidence before asking to speak to someone in authority, you give yourself authority. Telemarketers may act as if they know you and rudely demand: "Is this Susan?" But in professional situations, it is more impressive to state your name, then ask to speak to whomever you wish to talk with. If you sound nervous or bored, the receptionist will pick up on it.

Other techniques: Make notes and follow them. Be organized, and don't lead off with too much background. Limit the scope of the call; those who try to say everything say nothing. Close with your call to action or request. A little repetition is fine, but save the small talk for the golf course. Visualize every phone conversation as an inverted pyramid. Open with the main message and fill in supporting detail as needed. Be ready to cut and run if the person on the other end suddenly needs to exit—or another call cuts in.

Voice and Text Messages

To leave a cogent voice or text message, the same principles apply. State who you are and why you are contacting this person. Say what you want and when you need it. Be brief. Be even more brief. Include contact information even though they may have it. And for voice messages, slow down when giving the contact information. Make things easier for whoever you are communicating with, and they will be more likely to help you.

TELEPHONE TIPS AND TECHNIQUES

1. Write down points you want to cover ahead of time.
2. With authority, say: "Hello, this is_____. Is _____ available?"
3. Smile as you speak.
4. Pace your words to the speed of the person on the other end.
5. Restate complex information.
6. Actively listen as the other person speaks.
7. Leave your phone number, e-mail, other contact information—and timelines.
8. If you say you will call back, do so.

E-Mail Etiquette

As an e-mail writer, you not only decide what to say and how to say it, but who to say it to. The ease of sending messages to multiple audiences is a blessing and a curse, as anyone who receives multiple FWDs (forwarded messages) can attest. All businesspeople with computers complain that they get too much e-mail. Therefore, only send yours to those busy people who are directly involved—most specifically, those who will make decisions about that project. Sometimes it's politic to copy other people, but address the communication to as few people as possible. Like phone calls, e-mails come across with more energy when you can imagine the face of the person to whom you are writing, and they are many times more effective.

Once you have culled your list of recipients to only those people who can make decisions about or implement the project, follow the 12 Steps for Effective Writing on page 93, with special emphasis on steps seven and eight. And be brief. This is *electronic* mail; speed is its reason for being. Long e-mails are oxymoronic—and depressing.

However, *The Business Writer's Handbook* advises: "[A]lthough you want to keep sentences brief and words short, you should not use a telegraphic style that leaves important information unsaid—or only partly said. . . . Because email messages are recorded . . . they could be read or printed by someone other than the intended recipient."[9]

And you should always identify the subject of an e-mail—preferably in five words or less, precise and inviting. Recipients then may choose *not* to read that particular e-mail, but that's a chance you take. At any rate, in the world of audit-related e-mails, the surprise factor is not a plus.

Here are a couple of faulty samples of typical internal audit–related e-mails, accompanied by revised versions to use as positive examples.

Faulty Sample 1

Attached per your request is an analysis of Q2 AP Trade Payables split between FI Documents and PO Documents. The analysis recaps posting of dollars based on:

- Invoices dated previous period but posted in subsequent period

- Invoices dated same period and posted same period

- Percentages for each

Feel free to contact me if you need the detail supporting these dollars or questions regarding the spreadsheet itself.

Even though this e-mail appears superficially well-organized and audience-directed with its bullet points and references to the recipient, it can be improved significantly. The version below jettisons the overused "per your request" and actually clarifies the meaning of the two kinds of invoices. Most important, it sets a deadline for further involvement:

Attached is the analysis of Q2 AP Trade Payables split between Invoice Documents and Purchase Orders, which you requested.

The posting of dollars is based on two categories: (1) invoices dated previous period but posted in subsequent period, and (2) invoices dated and posted same period. The percentages for each category are also reflected.

Please contact me by COB Friday if you need supporting detail or have questions regarding the spreadsheet.

E-mail chains can be unending unless time frames are specifically stated, and many businesspeople lose interest in a subject after the first couple of e-mails. The preceding version prioritizes and clarifies the message, and gives the recipient a sense of impending completion.

But notice how this next faulty sample starts.

Faulty Sample 2

Yesterday I had a meeting with the accountants in Mexico to discuss the support we might need to smooth the month-end process. Some of the topics covered in that meeting were questions about whether or not to capitalize customs duties and circumstances under which payroll reclassifications should occur. It was decided that in the case of customs duties on purchases to third parties, we need the PO number captured in the system so that items purchased can be readily identified. Moving the close of the PO system 24 hours earlier would also be beneficial. Please research the steps necessary to reschedule the PO system closing and get back to me asap.

Too much background or too much nonessential information at the beginning ruins many a memo or e-mail. And the writer committed the capital crime: burying the lead. The most important points should always be stated first; then, if action is required, the request should be specific. "ASAP" and "soon" are, mercifully, shorter than "in a timely manner," but just as vague. E-mail writers do recipients a favor by helping them decide when they need to attend to a specific request. A revision of sample 2 could look something like this:

Please find out what steps are necessary to reschedule the PO system closing and get back to me no later than COB Friday, June 5.

In the case of customs duties on purchases to third parties, we need to capture PO numbers in the system so that items purchased can be readily identified. And closing the PO system 24 hours earlier would alleviate the last-minute panic.

These two recommendations came out of a meeting I had yesterday with the accountants in Mexico to discuss how we might smooth the month-end process. Two of the other topics covered were questions about whether or not to capitalize customs duties and circumstances under which payroll reclassifications should occur.

Your help on this is appreciated. Let me know if you have questions.

Although it makes logical, linear sense to start at the beginning of an issue and proceed step by step to the present, when time is short and attention spans shorter, e-mail recipients need to know what is expected of them right away, exactly what they need to do, and when. Then, if they get called to another country before they finish reading your missive, at least they can be thinking about your request as they go through those airport security lines.

Every call to action requires a deadline, as well as a specific request. Sometimes people think they are being pushy by specifying a time limit, but in fact, it is much easier for busy people to triage their work—or at least file their "to do" items chronologically. "Let me know soon" is not nearly as effective as "I need this information no later than Tuesday at 5 p.m. And many thanks."

One primary subject per e-mail is another effective technique. Asking too many things in one send often results in getting answers to only part of the questions. It's better to focus each e-mail on a specific outcome.

Technologist Paul Mansfield sums up what makes e-mail effective: "If you want to be read, you must resonate with your reader. Carefully craft each message, and use timing to your advantage. Doing business is about relationship building. Don't waste your customer or potential customer's time with long-winded verbiage. Write only when you have relevant information to convey, and get right to the point."[10]

E-MAIL TIPS AND TECHNIQUES

1. Address e-mails only to the decision makers and copy as few people as possible. Get names and titles right, and list them alphabetically—or politically.
2. Identify the subject precisely, and avoid multiple subjects.
3. Make the opening sentence do most of the work.
4. Skip unnecessary background, and get to the point.
5. Make it look good.
6. If you want action, make your expectation specific and supply a deadline.
7. Read it over at least once before clicking SEND.
8. Don't e-mail when you're angry.

Notes

1. John Seely Brown and Paul Duguid, *The Social Life of Information* (Boston: Harvard Business School Press, 2002).
2. *Internal Auditing's Role in Sections 302 and 404 of the U.S. Sarbanes-Oxley Act of 2002,* The Institute of Internal Auditors, Altamonte Springs, FL, May 26, 2004.
3. Cynthia Harrington, *Internal Audit's New Role, www.aicpa.org/pubs/jofa/sep2004/harring.htm.*
4. Robert E. Lefton, Ph.D., telephone interview from Venice, Italy, June 6, 2006.
5. Robert E. Lefton, Ph.D., and Victor R. Buzzotta, Ph.D., *Leadership Through People Skills* (New York: McGraw-Hill, 2004). Copyright by Psychological Associates, Inc.
6. Robert E. Lefton, Ph.D, telephone interview, June 6, 2006.
7. PCAOB, Bylaws and Rules-Standards-AS2, Section 81.
8. Marshall Rosenberg, Founder and Director of the Center for Nonviolent Communication, *www.cnvc.org.*
9. Charles T. Brusaw, Gerald J. Alred, and Walter E. Oliu, *The Business Writer's Handbook,* 5th ed. (New York: St. Martin's Press, 1997).
10. Paul Mansfield, New Mexico Technologist, *www.paulconsults.com,* e-mail correspondence, June 4, 2006.

REPORT WRITING 101, ER, MAKE THAT 404

Writing about business is not much different from covering a plane crash or a hockey game—you have to find out what happened, then explain it clearly.

The Associated Press Stylebook and Libel Manual

In the wake of Sarbanes-Oxley, executives must formally attest to the accuracy and completeness of their financial reports. Therefore, they need to completely read those reports and quickly grasp the full import of the findings and recommendations. Therefore, it's time for a crash course in cranking up the readability of internal audit reports.

Even when automated reporting software, covered in Chapters 3 and 4, is available, an observant, nonautomated entity needs to "write" the information into a coherent, complete report. Computers are not always adept at noticing what was left out, and if the input data is garbage, then the output will be garbage, too.

Anyone with a keen eye for details and discrepancies—and that certainly includes internal auditors—can write. The classic volume *On Writing Well* (an especially useful book for nonnative English speakers) includes a chapter titled "Nonfiction as the New American Literature." In it, author William Zinsser acknowledges the legitimacy of all the authors who routinely write about real-world subjects, including business. But putting report writing in the category of literature doesn't mean that internal auditors need to get drunk and come up with creative ways of stating conclusions. Auditors simply need to convey knowledge, as opposed to mere data, that is "clearly presented and thoughtfully arranged." That's what this section of the process is all about: how to communicate so that the meaning is laser-sharp and the logic compelling, and how to write and package reports so that people want to read them.

The next four chapters are cumulative. Beginning with the criteria for making the right report-writing decisions, they progress from individual word choices through sentence construction and paragraph structure to the final edit. In order to be sure those automated programs are effective, auditors need to know what good writing looks like. Chapter 6 lists three primary decision criteria, followed by best practices for verbs, precise words, and conciseness. Chapter 7 deals with effective sentences, the correct placement of modifiers, and which prepositions to choose. Paragraph structure and punctuation are the subjects of Chapter 8, and Chapter 9 completes the readability picture with a review of graphic elements and various editing techniques. Reports that look good reflect high-quality auditing work.

First, a few words of inspiration—and 12 steps that, when followed, produce the kind of reports that audit committees, CAEs, and managers value.

An old Italian proverb says: Think much, speak little, write less.

Tips and Techniques

A 12-Step Program for Effective Writing

1. Be clear about the message. Know your stuff.

2. Know your audience. Analyze their needs.

3. Key in whatever comes to mind without having to make it perfect—this includes prepackaged, automated information. Rearrange, cut and paste, and group related thoughts. Delete unnecessary ideas.

4. Organize and outline the material. (You are now ready to actually "write.")

5. Choose precise, direct words—only as many as absolutely needed. Feel free to edit the automation.

6. Make sure verbs agree with their subjects in number—and don't turn verbs into nouns. Use simple tenses.

7. Make sentences active and keep subjects as close to verbs as possible.

8. Limit sentences to one main idea; be sure that modifying phrases are positioned properly.

9. Keep paragraphs short and related to the topic sentence, which should be the first sentence. Use transition words to reinforce the logic.

10. Punctuate sentences to improve understanding. (Concentrate on commas.)

11. Use graphics where appropriate. A chart can be worth a thousand words.

12. Proofread everything at least once. Schedule time for this task. Then edit and rewrite as much as possible. This step makes the difference between "uh-oh!" and ready to go.

CHAPTER 6

CRITICAL WORD
CHOICES

Writing is a decision-making process. Just as audit report content decisions are based on legal requirements (e.g., Sarbanes-Oxley, the SEC), professional standards (e.g., the IIA, AICPA), and business needs (the company being audited, the audit committee, the stakeholders), writing decisions should be based on specific criteria.

WORD CHOICE CRITERIA

Deciding *how* to say what you have decided to say should be based on:

1. *The most effective way to communicate with the individuals who will read and attest to the report*—what will satisfy the CEO and audit committee
2. *Generally accepted usage, formats, and style conventions in the corporate culture being audited*—what the CAE and audit manager look for
3. *The rules of punctuation and grammar*—what maximizes credibility and makes for faster comprehension

Taking Account of the Audience

Since SOX, audit committees, audit executives, and internal auditors are finding themselves in closer contact. That heightened level of communication will make it easier to determine precisely what levels of risk, internal controls, and operational and technical information should be included in any particular report. In addition, identifying specific writing criteria that are most likely to succeed should be easier. Are the members of the audit committee detail-oriented (not "orientated")? Does the CAE insist on using (not "utilizing") certain phrases—and excluding others? Are the managers sticklers for particular punctuation conventions or currency notations?

Chapter 5 covered the conversational components of the audit process and suggested questions to ask and ways to get clear about what audit report recipients are looking for in terms of content. With respect to writing style preferences and formats, it's often a good idea to ask audit committees to indicate which of two or three formats they prefer. Informal audience surveys can also be used to confirm that the auditors and the company managers are, literally, on the same page. To settle questions about acceptable grammar, some audit departments supply previously well-written reports to their team; nothing beats a reliable model.

Professional writers generally submit articles to their editors only after discussing what is expected. Why should internal auditors think they need to go it alone? Auditors can still maintain professional independence and objectivity about the content—without operating in a vacuum about the best way to communicate it.

Another effective way to determine what readers will respond to best is by sending them, in advance, the proposed outline or Table of Contents. By involving the report recipients early on, the chances for cooperation during the audit process increase geometrically. An audience analysis checklist is included in Chapter 10.

Generally Accepted Usage

Generally accepted business usage (GABU?) varies from company to company—and from country to country. But in general, whatever requires the fewest keystrokes and gets the message across is preferable.

Twenty-first-century writing style is direct, intimate, and informal. Phrases such as "Please find enclosed as per your request" and "Should you have any questions or concerns, please feel free to call" are replaced by shorter ones: "Attached are" and "Please call if you have questions." In audit reports, the old boilerplate is updated by livelier, shorter statements of the scope and objectives.

Formal style guides about current writing styles are now provided by many corporations. Such stylistic conventions as what to capitalize, how to show currencies, and when and how to use footnotes with tables are just a few of the subjects dealt with, in addition to definitions of terms and recommended word use.

Knowing what is acceptable in each unique corporate context is a report-writing priority. A phrase that is acceptable and comprehensible in the United Kingdom may not translate to parts of the United States, even though people in both countries speak the same language! For example, using the word *scheme* to describe a business plan in the United States suggests a shady deal; however, *scheme* works fine in countries where the Queen's English is used. Professor Harold Hill in *The Music Man* was right: "You gotta know the territory."

A top-ten list of widely accepted style considerations follows:

TIPS AND TECHNIQUES *Top Ten Style Considerations*

1. Keep reports short and always include an Executive Summary.
2. Be consistent with terminology.
3. Use headings and subheadings to make documents more accessible.
4. Spell out all acronyms when first used in a document.
5. Spell out numbers one through nine.
6. Make subjects like "auditors" plural to avoid gender exclusiveness.
7. Avoid using complex words when natural, direct words are available.

(continued)

TIPS AND TECHNIQUES *(continued)*

---

8. Follow standard rules of punctuation (e.g., when and when not to use commas).

9. Use tables and graphs to communicate complex data sets.

10. Follow standard grammar rules.

Note: The preceding style considerations apply to both SOX-specific reports and to traditional financial and operations audit reports. Just because automated dashboards and other sophisticated tools are used, does not relieve auditors of their oversight responsibilities regarding accurate words.

Grammar on the Rocks

The word *grammar* has long had a bad rap, probably because of its association with the word "school." But following grammatical conventions is actually no more difficult than adhering to auditing standards. Of course, both sets of rules are changing.

What is grammatically correct in the twenty-first century? Will ending a sentence with a preposition irritate this particular manager? Can you start a sentence with "but"? What constitutes good grammar in an audit report that follows a tabular format? What if the automated report verbiage sounds awkward?

Many books have been written on the subject of grammar, and some are listed in Appendix C. However, because grammar rules are changing almost as fast as cell phone options, it's a good idea to refer to publications such as the *Wall Street Journal* and *The Economist* to stay on top of how business people are using English words.

For instance, it's now permissible to end sentences with prepositions, to split infinitives, and to start sentences with "and" and "but." Here's William Zinsser's take on "but": "Many of us were taught that no sentence should begin with 'but.' If that's what you learned, unlearn it—there is no stronger word at the start. It announces total contrast with what has gone before, and the reader is primed for the change."[1]

In terms of how the words are changing, *impact* has become a verb as well as a noun, and *data* (actually the plural of "datum") is considered singular. Several more taboos will probably have been broken by the time this book is printed.

Here, however, are five rock-solid grammar rules with respect to verbs, the most important words in every sentence. When writing reports that will be read by discriminating readers, focus on the verb.

RULES OF THE VERB

Numero Uno: Make Sure the Subject and the Verb Agree in Number

No, not that kind of number—singulars (one entity) and plurals (more than one). If the subject is singular, the form of the verb needs to be singular too. For example:

> "Authorization for payroll changes was not given."
>
> Not: "Authorization for payroll changes were not given."

In the second version, perhaps the writer focused on the word "changes," realized it was plural, and went on to choose the plural verb "were." But, the subject of that verb is actually "authorization," a singular noun.

Audit reports tend to be composed of (not "comprised of") many sentences with complex thoughts and phrases, and picking out the subject from among the numerous noun suspects can be tricky. For example:

> *Authorization* for payroll changes to the master file made in the last quarter because of layoffs **was not given.**

Many nouns are present: layoff, the last quarter, the master file, the payroll changes, but the subject is still "authorization."

The important step in this process is to identify the *subject* and the **verb.** Regardless of how many modifying phrases are present, the basic elements in this example are: *Authorization* . . . **was not given.**

Here's a typical standards statement to decipher; for purposes of this exercise, just ask yourself whether the verb "suggests" is used properly.

> Even though some requirements of this standard are set forth in a manner that suggests a sequential process, auditing internal control over financial reporting involves a process of gathering, updating, and analyzing information.

Answer? Yes, the verb "suggests" refers back to the word "manner" and is used correctly.

Here's one more example:

> Based on public record data, CAPEX as a percentage of revenues were on average four points higher over the last ten years.

Correct? Of course not. The subject is CAPEX. A singular, though collective, noun.

The sentence should read:

> Based on public record data, *CAPEX*, as a percentage of revenues **was**, on average, four points higher than ten years ago.

Note: In American English, collective nouns are treated as singular entities. General Motors is, the audit committee is, the IIA is. But mind your verbs when in UK-governed cultures. The Queen's English dictates that collectives be treated as plurals. British Aerospace are, the IIA are.

Numero Dos: Use Active Voice, the Active Form of the Verb, Whenever Possible

If the first example about payroll authorization had been written in the active voice, the subject would have been named, and the sentence would have been written like this:

> The *supervisors* **did not authorize** payroll changes.

But in the original example, perhaps the auditors did not wish to accuse the supervisors directly and so chose the passive voice.

Here's another example:

> The *finance department* **reviewed** the documents.

Not:

The documents were reviewed by the finance department.

The complete rule is: Use active voice except when defusing the message would be politically correct, which is just as important as being grammatically correct.

Active voice is also beneficial because it shortens the sentence, makes the meaning easier to grasp, and makes the writing more lively.

Most software packages will flag verbs in the passive voice, and they are often easy to identify because of the presence of the preposition "by." The action was done "by" someone or some group. Those squiggly green or red lines constitute an early-warning system for unintended lapses into passivity—so, no excuses for unconsciously wilting the words!

Numero Tres: Don't Make Verbs into Nouns

Another bad habit in much business writing is reducing the potency of verbs by making them into nouns. These nasty nominalizations usually occur when a suffix, such as –ion or –ment, is added to what was formerly a vital verb. Making verbs into nouns really bogs down the writing—and the reading.

VERB TIPS AND TECHNIQUES

Bogged Down Noun	*Dynamic Verb*
Make a recommendation	Recommend
Reach a decision	Decide
Formulate a plan	Plan
Make an allocation	Allocate
Perform a calculation	Calculate

As the following examples illustrate, what works best is to "cut to the chase":

We *agreed* to list the revenues.

Not: We made an agreement to list the revenues.

Internal audit **reconciled** the two accounts.

Not: Internal audit made a reconciliation of the differences between the two accounts.

Numero Quattro: Use Simple Tenses

The following example shows two versions of the same sentence, but the first one is shorter, and more satisfying, in that the reader doesn't wonder what might have been left out. Had they included an advance but decided to remove it?

They *included* an advance of USD xxx in the account.

Not: They had included an advance of USD xxx in the account.

It can be a jolt for romance language natives to shift to such harsh-sounding, to their ears, Anglo-Saxon syllables, but using simple tenses saves keystrokes and makes meanings clearer.

The Verb Tenses table in Exhibit 6.1 shows preferred verb forms in bold type.

Exhibit 6.1 *Verb Tenses*

Past	**I wrote**
Past Perfect	I had written
Present	**I write**
Present Perfect	I have written
Future	**I will write**
Future Perfect	I will have written

Just for the record, the **past perfect tense** is used when one past event precedes another, for example:

> He *had written* the report by the time the CAE arrived.

The **present perfect tense** describes something from the recent past that is related to the present, such as:

> They **have written** the first draft of the report and are ready to begin revising it.

And the **future perfect tense** indicates action that will have been completed at a time in the future, for example:

> They **will have rewritten** the presentation three times by the time they review it with the audit committee.

The general rule on tense is: Be consistent. If the verb in the main clause (the stand-alone part of the sentence) is in the past tense, the verb in the subordinate clause (the expendable part) should also be in the past tense. If the findings included in a paragraph were discovered in the past and relate to past conditions, the whole paragraph—generally—should be written using past tense. Because audit findings are by nature events and data observed in the past, most statements in an internal audit report—with the exception of the recommendations—will be written in the past tense.

Final Numero (Not Really a Rule, but a Fine Idea): Use Parallel Structure

Parallel structure means setting up sentences so that related thoughts are expressed in similar ways, using similar word order.

Notice, in the following example, that the payment was made to accomplish two things: clean the warehouse and treat the water.

> A *payment* of USD 67,000 **was made** in December 2004 to clean the warehouse and treat the polluted water and mud.

In the following nonparallel version, the meaning is delayed, the water treatment sounds like an afterthought, and the impact is lessened.

> Not: A payment of USD 67,000 was made in December 2004 to clean the warehouse and for the treatment of polluted water and mud.

Parallel structure makes the logic of what is being said explicit and, therefore, lessens the mental effort required by a busy executive.

Speaking of reducing mental effort, the term *respectively* is not effective in that regard. It's a rather old-fashioned term, used perhaps by writers who want to sound stylish. Adding just a few more words improves clarity and comprehension, and sounds even more impressive.

Consider these examples, and lose "respectively":

> Internal audit determined that sales were USD 450,000 in September 2006 and USD 750,000 in December 2006.

> Not: Internal audit determined that sales were USD 450,000 and USD 750,000 in September 2006 and December 2006, respectively.

> For the comparable period this year, rates of change were 5% for Accounts Receivable and 15% for Accounts Payable.

> Not: Rates of change for the comparable period this year were 5% and 15% respectively for Account Receivable and Accounts Payable.

Just for fun (this is my idea of fun?), Appendix B contains a series of Find-the-Flaw exercises in which to test your keen observation and merciless editing skills. The first 10 sentences contain errors with respect to verbs, and, for all of us instant gratification junkies, corrections immediately follow.

PRECISE AND SPECIFIC WORDS

Nothing deadens writing more than vague generalities, even if they are grammatically correct and well punctuated. Likewise, nothing frustrates CAEs and managers more than the same tired abstractions, accurately, but arduously, presented.

On the contrary, nothing elicits a positive response from IA executives—and makes a convincing case for changing company procedures—better than specific recommendations expressed in words that create images in the mind.

Consider the following:

> Prior to uploading in the accounting system, the payroll file should be reviewed and approved by the personnel manager, and payroll details should be provided to the directors of departments on a monthly basis so that they can be reviewed and validated.

Nothing in the preceding sentence is incorrect, but nothing motivates a reader to take action either. Look at this snazzier version:

> The personnel manager should review the payroll file before it is uploaded to MFG/Pro, and department directors should review and validate payroll costs monthly.

By focusing right away on who should do what—and exactly what, MfgPro, not "the accounting system,"—and by getting rid of extraneous words, the second version makes the recommendation sound eminently more do-able.

If a recommendation merely says: "Cash receipts should be recorded properly," the statement is correct as far as it goes. However, the meaning of "properly" is not made clear. Can these transactions be handled by anyone on staff? The recommendation should be: "Cash receipts should be recorded correctly by the appropriate accountants, not by the same employees who handle cash or checks."

Precise words are as important as precise figures; items on the balance sheet are not listed using approximate amounts. By the way, don't say "amount" (quantities in mass but not discrete items that can be counted) when you really mean "number" (how many); and don't refer to "data" (facts or figures to be processed, evidence, records, statistics) when you are dealing with "information" (data that is gathered by reading or observation and does not necessarily connote validity).

CODE WORDS AND ACRONYMS

The value of using consistent terminology and spelling out acronyms cannot be overstated. As American humorist Will Rogers wisely noted:

"It isn't what we don't know that gets us into trouble, it's what we know—that just ain't so."

The SOX legislation and its related directives from regulatory and professional organizations have generated numerous new terms; therefore, definitions and meanings need to be repeatedly clarified until, in fact, the meanings are clear! Ongoing discussion is recommended about exactly what is implied by—and inferred from—terms such as: "COSO framework," "nonaudit services," and "reasonable assurance." With respect to Section 404 compliance, Richard M. Steinberg, founder and principal of Steinberg Governance Advisors, pointed out the importance of uniform language: "Companies have learned that communicating across the organization is hampered when employees have very different meanings for the same words."[2]

Acronyms can be ambiguous, as well as misleading. One seminar of physicians and nurses insisted they knew what all the medical acronyms meant, but half the group said DOA meant Dead on Arrival, and the other half said it meant Date of Admission. In an audit, not spelling out the acronym might mean the difference, in a moment of short attention span, between assuming SAS referred to a software company instead of a professional standard. The rule is: Always spell out the acronym the first time it is referenced, with the spelled-out term followed by the acronym in parentheses. Then the acronym will suffice throughout the rest of the document.

THE IMPORTANCE OF BEING SPECIFIC

Auditors who make precise and specific statements about their findings get precise and specific responses. But that was a rather general statement, so let me be specific. The abstract, editorial words in the following example should be replaced by quantifiable, objective ones:

> Insufficient documentation was kept by the Purchasing Department and they failed to show receipt of goods in a timely manner. Several POs were not authorized.

"Insufficient documentation," "in a timely manner," and "several" are all abstract, vague terms. You cannot draw a picture of any of them.

"Insufficient" and "timely" are also editorial in that they represent opinion, not demonstrable fact. And add the phrase "they failed" to the mix, and you have the potential for fightin' words.

A more effective way to state that finding is:

> To show receipt of goods, the Purchasing Department maintained only Delivery Letters and Shipping Documents which were over three months old. Twenty-five unauthorized Purchase Orders (POs) were found in a separate file.

The managers may not be happy with that finding, but it will be difficult to argue with quantifiable facts.

Professional writers are often reminded to say "a rose," not "a flower." Ditto for auditors with respect to "delivery letters," not "documentation." By stating only what is observable, quantifiable, and specific, tone and clarity are improved, and the possibility of offending someone by making an arbitrary comment is avoided.

One advantage of typical SOX audit formats is that they usually list specific findings. Then the auditor can quickly summarize, without editorializing, and "communicate" to the audit committee and management what they need to know.

A tip regarding "dead" writing: Once particular phrases are written down or keyed into a document, dislodging those words becomes more difficult. As notes are taken and work papers filled out during testing, write down specific phrases and expressions that are lively and have an impact. Spare yourself the boredom of repeating tired abstractions when you are trying to reconstitute what was observed. Use the energy of the on-site immediacy to record significant information—using real words, the ones you and everybody else related to during the fieldwork.

CONCISENESS

The term *conciseness* is often misinterpreted. Conciseness is not a numbers game and does not mean merely shorter, but rather, complete in as few words as possible. To put it in auditing terms, being concise means making every word count. Sometimes the most concise way to say something actually requires a few more words. For example, the terse, telegraphic style popularized by e-mail can sometimes leave out salient details, necessitating even more e-mail.

More frequently, auditors expand basic ideas into complicated phrases and lose the narrative storyline of their report. If all the detailed tests and every possible qualification of every point are included in a report, the subject will certainly be covered. But no one will read what was written.

Effective auditors articulate observations and recommendations so that audit committees are impressed by the value of their report—not the volume—and will be more inclined to agree with the findings.

The easiest way to produce value-not-volume reports is to eliminate the seven deadly sins (well, bad habits) that obliterate conciseness:

1. Repetition and redundancy
2. Lack of subordination[3]
3. Passive voice
4. Wordy phrases
5. Expletives ("there are" and "it is"—not the other kind!)
6. Overuse of adjectives, adverbs, and qualifiers
7. Writing to impress more than express

Expressing the same idea in different words is *repetition*. In the following examples, the italicized words are unnecessary:

> In fifty percent of the files tested, payments to customer files were missing *or unable to be located*.

> Twenty-first century internal auditors *of today* are more knowledgeable about IT issues than their predecessors.

Redundancy means using another word, usually an adjective, to describe a word that already conveys the meaning of the adjective. Again, the italicized words are unnecessary in the following examples:

> Assets should be *adequately* safeguarded.

> *Advance* planning is needed to safeguard the assets.

> The *final* outcome surpassed the plan.

Lack of subordination occurs when a main idea is expressed, followed by a supporting idea expressed with equal weight. For example:

> The internal audit report was carefully organized, *and it covered twenty pages.*

By integrating the qualifying words describing the length of the report, the sentence is made more concise, and the supporting idea is subordinated to the main idea.

> The twenty-page internal audit report was carefully organized.

Passive voice was discussed in the section on verbs, but the following example demonstrates the literary virtue of conciseness:

> The Fixed Assets listing is reviewed by Internal Audit on a monthly basis in order to ascertain whether or not capitalizations are being recorded properly, i.e., that only allowable items are capitalized.

By beginning the sentence with the subject, the tendency to run on is curbed, and conciseness is achieved.

> Each month, Internal Audit reviews the Fixed Assets listing to ensure that only allowable items are capitalized.

Wordy phrases are often the results of habit. So many reports have been written using extra words that the circumlocution (talking around) often sounds okay because it is familiar, but consider this example:

> For accounting and booking purposes, at the end of each week, please batch copies of checks with the supporting documents and send them to the Accounts Payable Department in order to ensure proper filing as soon as all the documentation arrives every week.

By focusing on the main message, eliminating extra words, and being more specific, this repetitive sentence can be significantly shortened and clarified.

> Every Friday, please batch copies of checks with supporting documents and send them to the Accounts Payable Department to ensure timely filing.

Expletives. Do not begin sentences with "There is, there are, it is, it was," or use the relative pronoun "this" as in: "This means . . . this results in . . ." Name the thing even if the word has been used already. In the following example, what does "this" refer to?

> Internal audit reviewed 75 of 100 loans in the portfolio, 25 of which were found to be in compliance. This indicates a need for increased due diligence.

This discrepancy? This review? Defining the relative pronoun clarifies the meaning, and a more specific recommendation than "increased due diligence" would be helpful!

Overuse of adjectives, adverbs, and other qualifiers. Wordiness should never survive rewrite! The most effective way to write concisely is to mercilessly review what has been written—preferably aloud.

The italicized words in the following example add nothing material to the meaning; in fact, they subtract value and should be deleted:

> *As a result of* Internal Audit's review of Accounts Payable, *it was* noted that seven accounts were not included on the Cash Control listing *despite the fact* that those *very* important accounts were documented as being included.

The qualifying phrase "As a result of" is not needed because the context of the report would have conveyed that information; ditto for "it was." And the second qualifier, "despite the fact" is simply TMI. "Very" is an intensifier that adds nothing and should be avoided in business writing.

As has just been demonstrated, a sure way to make reports more concise is to take a hard look at all the prepositional phrases and decide whether they are essential. Prepositions will be covered in Chapter 7.

Finally, conciseness can be achieved by using *simpler words*. Multisyllable, spelling bee stumpers are not justified when simple words get the message across. No less a writer than Shakespeare (in *Henry V*) simply said: "Old men forget." He did *not* say: "Male persons of advanced years have a tendency to lose control of their recollective faculties." Internal audit reports should make a point, not an impression. The following example loses sight of the primary communication objective—being understood:

> Subsequent investigation revealed that the risk potential was significantly greater, vis-à-vis the preceding year's Receivables.

RIGHT WORD TIPS AND TECHNIQUES

Instead of:	*Try this:*
Aggregate	Total
Commence, initiate	Begin
Demonstrate, indicate	Show
Finalize, terminate	End
Methodology	Practice, method
Modification	Change
Personnel	People
Prior to	Before
Subsequent to	After, following
Utilize	Use

Try this instead:

> A follow-up review showed the risk potential in Receivables was fifty percent higher than last year.

Unfortunately, business writers often pick up bad language habits from their colleagues and surroundings. "This was in the last report," or "I saw this in a memo from the CAE, it must be right." A better way to decide what is appropriate is to question whatever sounds awkward—and get a second opinion from the boss!

No one wants to read ponderous prose. Busy executives are far more impressed by clarity and precision than they are by vocabulary and volume.

THE "WHATEVER" STEP

Step Three in the 12-Step Writing Program needs a bit of explanation. Where many report writers go wrong is in assuming that, once they have made it through the rigors of the audit process and decided what to say, they should be able to just sit down and write smooth-flowing sentences that morph into logically organized reports. They expect to complete the entire report in one pass—an impossible feat that professional writers would not even attempt.

The key to superior writing is, for a brief time, to drop the need to write everything perfectly and just allow words to take shape on the screen—right, wrong, misspelled, whatever. This "whatever step" is powerful. Key in whatever comes to mind, dump core, incorporate any automated inputs.

When you have exhausted your "outputs," write one or two lines that summarize the main message. Like the loglines screenwriters use to pitch their scripts to Hollywood producers, this brief summary is the main message to be delivered, and everything included in the report should support it. Then organize, list priorities, jot an outline. After that, you are ready to compose sentences, which are covered in the next chapter.

Notes

1. William Zinsser, *On Writing Well*, 3rd ed. (New York: Harper & Row, 1985), p. 143.
2. Richard M. Steinberg, "Resources, Ownership and Discipline: Key 404 Lessons," *Compliance Week*. October 18, 2005.
3. Charles T. Brusaw, Gerald J. Alred, and Walter E. Oliu, *The Business Writer's Handbook*, 5th ed. (New York: St. Martin's Press, 1997).

CHAPTER 7

STRUCTURED SENTENCES

Reviews of internal controls proceed logically and systematically, and so should every sentence that "communicates the engagement results." In English sentences, the placement of the words matters. What comes first is perceived as more important, and what follows needs to be subordinated so that the relationships between the ideas are clear.

But, in the real world, auditors rarely schedule enough time to review their sentences with the same sharp observational skills they use in reviewing potential areas of risk. And many auditors work in teams spread out in cyberspace, so they tend to write reports—and sentences—on the run.

Speaking of running on, if three people in geographically diverse locations are writing an internal audit report conclusion via e-mail, there is a good chance that their sentences will sound patched together like this one, which continues aggregating what come across as afterthoughts, even though the words make sense, but somehow never satisfies the reader either because of the complexity and sheer number of words or the loss of focus on the main idea. (Does the verb "satisfies" refer back to words or sentence?)

Regardless of new software programs that almost write the report automatically—and, in some cases, because of sophisticated high-tech tools—new methods of managing report production are needed.

Delegation of specific segments and ample discussion of how those segments fit together will improve sentence construction, as well as streamline the whole report process. Most important, the readability rules of unity and coherence should be communicated to and practiced by everyone on the team.

Sentence unity and coherence are not that hard to come by. Focusing on the subject and the predicate comes first. Arrangement of the words in the appropriate order is next. And an enthusiastic willingness to change the prepositions, move the modifiers, or delete any phrase that is not essential completes the process.

Just as the templates in Chapter 4 provided a visual roadmap for main messages, the "sentence schemata" in this chapter (not to be confused with boring grammar school diagrams!) illustrate the structure of sentences. Tips on achieving conciseness, avoiding wordiness, and understanding prepositional relationships (that sounds weird) are also included.

IDENTIFYING THE SUBJECT

The run-on sentence is the most common mistake in business writing. Even if technically and grammatically correct, long sentences annoy readers and reduce credibility. Why? Because readers have to work hard to make sense of long sentences. The auditors know what they observed, they were there, on the scene, but the report readers weren't. At the end of too many long sentences, if they reach the end, readers may doubt what they thought they read. (Recall the unsatisfying sentence in the preceding section.) They may not cop to it, but most people, at all levels in companies and organizational hierarchies, are slowed down, if not stopped, by convoluted sentences that require large quantities of personal interpretation.

To avoid run-on sentences, focus on the subject and the predicate, and only add supporting detail as absolutely necessary.

The basic elements of any sentence are:

- The **subject** (the do-er, or, in passive construction, that to which something is done)
- The **predicate** (what is done, for what reason, by whom)

Sometimes the predicate consists of only a verb:

I came. I saw. I conquered.

Without getting into too many grammar rules, the most important thing when structuring sentences is to give the subject prominence. Subjects are often buried in a matrix of complex phrases, which in turn deal with layers of complicated information. It is relatively easy to compose such sentences; people with only superficial knowledge of a subject can do it. But it takes mastery to explain complex information in simple, coherent terms. Making subjects easy to identify is one way for internal auditors to demonstrate that they really know what they are writing about.

To test your subject ID IQ, pick out the subjects in these three sentences:

1. Therefore, justification for the CAPEX in terms of asset utilization, financial return, or asset replacement is documented biannually in accordance with the requirements.

Right, the subject is "justification" not CAPEX, utilization, return, or replacement.

2. Included in the documentation provided for the December 2006 due diligence was a marketing agreement between the two entities, neither of which are located in Bangalore.

"Marketing agreement" is the subject, of course. When this sentence is analyzed visually (see page 121) the main idea emerges—that is, a marketing agreement was included in the documentation. All the other information simply adds detail to the main idea.

3. A deposit of USD 5 million from the manufacturer and an advance of USD 7.5 million from the parts supplier were combined, resulting in a customer deposit of USD 12.5 million.

Here, the subject is compound: "deposit" (of USD 5 million) and "advance" (of USD 7.5 million). Had the word order been reversed, for example, "A customer deposit of USD 12.5 million consisted of a deposit and an advance," then "customer deposit" would be the subject. This sentence is visualized on page 120.

OTHER SENTENCE COMPONENTS

In addition to having readily identifiable subjects and predicates, sentences should be constructed with a single idea, coherence, variety, parallelism, and active voice.

A *single idea* focuses thought and gives busy readers a break. In the wake of SOX, the tendency is to cover the bases so thoroughly that no salient point is unexamined and reported on. But that desire to leave no finding behind can create a problem when it comes to effectively communicating what is most significant.

Here is a comment to the PCAOB that refers to the proposed requirement in the amendment to AU 543 that the principal auditor review another auditor's audit documentation:

> They (the commenters) objected because they were of the opinion such a review would impose an unnecessary cost and burden, given that the other auditor will have already reviewed the documentation in accordance with the standards established by the principal auditor.[1]

The way this sentence is structured, the subject is "they" and the predicate is "objected." But the details surrounding the verb, "the because clause," are what matter most, and "an unnecessary cost and burden" is meaningless until we know what that phrase refers to.

Here's a possible revision:

> Because the other auditors would have already reviewed the documentation according to standards established by the principal auditors, the commenters objected to the amendment on the grounds that it would create unnecessary work and cost money.

Placing "the because clause" at the beginning of the sentence guarantees that the reader will focus on that idea.

Coherence is achieved by placing modifiers close to what they modify and subjects and verbs as close together as possible. And, because the logic of the content is reinforced by this kind of structural logic, coherence increases credibility. Sentences that are coherent give readers—and writers—the satisfaction that the intended meaning has been successfully conveyed. The only real rule for writing coherent sentences is to keep related thoughts close to each other.

In some languages, the placement of the words is not an issue—Japanese, for example. In English, however, especially American Business English, the physical location of each word is critical. Just moving a phrase can change the meaning—or clarify it.

Consider the following sentence:

> An exception report is published monthly on the Web site, listing all assets that require manual intervention in order to correct the interface record, which will facilitate clearing of the suspense accounts.

Is the publication schedule the most important idea to be communicated? Does the interface record facilitate the objective of clearing the suspense accounts?

Here's a revised version:

> An exception report, which lists all assets that require manual intervention to correct the interface record, is published monthly on the Web site. This report facilitates clearing the suspense accounts.

The revised version focuses on the significance of the report rather than where and when it is published; it also effectively connects "manual intervention" with correcting "the interface record." And it emphasizes the bit about clearing the suspense accounts by positioning that thought within its own sentence.

Variety uses introductory phrases and smooth transitions to make writing readable. Just as the "Me Tarzan, you Jane" dialogue in the old *Tarzan* movies left a lot to be desired, an overly repetitive sentence structure can make otherwise relevant information sound unimportant and incomplete.

For best results, this example should be read aloud:

> A file should be kept by the administrative function. The file should include a copy of the user profile and related e-mail approvals from the Controller. An employee independent of the administrative function should review the user IDs on a monthly basis. All user IDs should be current and have standard user profile matrices unless otherwise authorized.

To keep energy and interest flowing, introductory phrases would invite the reader to continue, and transition words would reinforce the logic. Here's an improved version:

> For each user, the administrative function should keep a file that includes a copy of the user profile and related e-mail approvals from the Controller. Then, a non-administrative employee should review all user IDs monthly to confirm that they are current and, unless authorized, include standard user profile matrices.

Parallelism is another sentence component that reinforces logic; and parallelism offers the kind of repetition that can strengthen sentences. Using the same order of sentence elements and word forms also makes meanings easier to retain.

As you read the following, notice your reaction:

> Internal Audit examined how AMCO processed claims, focusing on the effectiveness of existing procedures, adequate provisions, and how long each settlement took.

Did you read it twice to be sure you got the message? Did you find the phrase "adequate provisions" somehow inadequate? That sentence is not parallel—or convincing—because the three items following "focusing" are not written using the same forms of the words. "Effectiveness" is a noun, "adequate" is an adjective, and "how long" is a question. And, much worse, the way "adequate provisions" is stated is inaccurate.

Isn't this sentence clearer—and more reassuring?

> Internal Audit examined how AMCO processed claims and focused on the effectiveness of existing procedures, the adequacy of provisions, and the length of settlements.

The revised version focuses on what internal audit focused on, the three nouns: effectiveness, adequacy, and length.

Parallel structure is essential when the theme-and-bullet-points format is used. Notice how these points come across:

For unbilled A/R, the following work was performed:

- Documents supporting the balance were obtained.

- Age verification was made of most significant Revenue accruals.

- On a sample basis, verified that necessary documents and signatures were obtained.

The facts are there, but the advantage of using the theme-and-bullets format is lost.

Look at this version:

For unbilled A/R, internal audit performed the following:

- Obtained documents supporting the balance

- Verified the age of the most significant Revenue accruals

- Verified, based on samples, that necessary documents and signatures were obtained

And the way the theme is stated in the revision, using active construction, "internal audit performed" is also the final sentence element.

Active voice makes sentences dynamic, as well as shorter. The distinction between active and passive verbs was covered in Chapter 6, but here are two more examples.

Is this crisp writing?

At the time of the review, there was no link between the authentication diskette and the user ID of a signatory.

When the subject is left out (and the expletive "there was" is left in!), the construction becomes passive and lifeless. Here's a revision:

Internal audit detected no link between the authentication diskette and the signatory's user ID.

More wilted writing:

> By looking at the expense line in the P&L and relating it back to inventory on hand in the balance sheet, the inventory days appeared to be below 90 days.

Look how much more effective the sentence becomes when you lead with the subject, instead of dragging through all the various steps.

> Inventory days appeared to be below 90 days, as determined by comparing the expense line in the P&L to inventory on hand in the balance sheet.

SENTENCE SCHEMATA

One practical, if not exactly high-tech, tool to help isolate the elements in any sentence is the diagram. Not those dreaded diagrams from grammar school or linguistics classes, but sleek twenty-first-century "schemata" that use ovoid shapes and can be deciphered fast (see Exhibit 7.1, Sentence One).

EXHIBIT 7.1 *Sentence One*

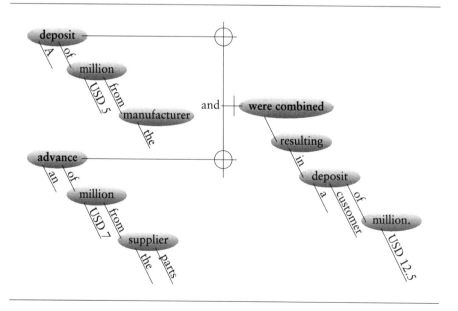

Undiagrammed, Sentence One reads as follows:

> A deposit of USD 5 million from the manufacturer and an advance of USD 7 million from the parts supplier were combined, resulting in a customer deposit of USD 12 million.

The schema isolates the subject—in this case a compound of two nouns—and predicate: *deposit and advance were combined*. The other elements, shown in the descending prepositional phrases, are then seen in their relationship to the main idea—and can be left in as needed.

Sentence Two (Exhibit 7.2), undiagrammed, reads:

> Therefore, justification for the capex in terms of asset utilization, financial return or asset replacement is documented biannually in accordance with the requirements.

EXHIBIT 7.2   *Sentence Two*

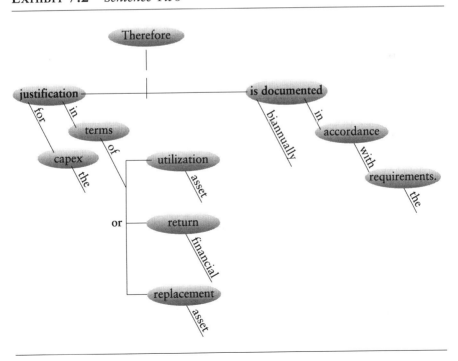

The basic elements? *Justification is documented.* All the rest of those words describe what sort of justification it is and how it is being documented.

A final sentence schema:

> A marketing agreement between the two entities, neither of which are located in Bangalore, was included in the documentation provided for the December 2005 due diligence.

Sentence Three (Exhibit 7.3) includes what amounts to an almost parenthetical remark, the bit about neither entity being located in Bangalore. Sometimes, such information carries weight and should be included, but always be sure such lengthy (an extra six words!) additions add value.

EXHIBIT 7.3   *Sentence Three*

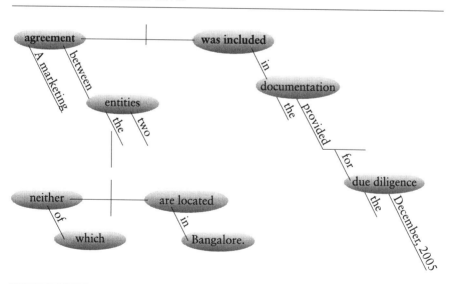

MOVING ON TO MODIFIERS

Grammatical disconnects reflect a lack of connection in the thought process, and they may suggest to managers a lack of connection in the audit process. So using modifiers to make the right connections between ideas is important. In *Modern American Usage*, Eric Wensberg urges writers to "connect modifiers and their objects in such a way that the resulting phrase slips into the mind without effort."[2]

Misplaced modifiers, sometimes referred to as "dangling modifiers," are one of the surest tip-offs to disconnected thought.

Sometimes misplaced modifiers can be funny:

> The 10-K reports were filed accidentally by an employee who had worked in the finance department for ten years in the wrong drawer.

To free the employee, the modifying phrase "in the wrong drawer" must be moved.

> The 10-K reports were filed, accidentally, in the wrong drawer by an employee who had worked in the finance department for ten years.

Most of the time, modifiers in the wrong place are merely confusing:

> We added the figures for premiums due on the spreadsheet and compared that total to several other totals.

Were premiums due on the spreadsheet? The best practice is to put any phrase that describes how the action was done, in this case, "on the spreadsheet," as close to the verb as possible.

> On the spreadsheet, we added the figures for premiums due and compared that total to several other totals.

Modifers Defined

What is a modifier? A phrase or word that limits or describes another word. Consider these three sentences that have only "only" as the modifier:

I *only* processed the report. (I didn't do anything else with it.)

Only I processed the report. (No one else did.)

I processed *only* the report. (I processed nothing else.)

Even though the same words are used, the meaning changes according to where the modifier "only" is placed.

The next two sentences also use the same words yet have different meanings because of where the modifier, "specifically," is placed:

> The exposure reports of September and December did not address any of the situations *specifically* outlined below; in many cases the risk was below the materiality threshold.

> The exposure reports of September and December did not *specifically* address any of the situations outlined below; in four of the five cases, the risk was below the materiality threshold.

Not only does the second example place the modifier more accurately, but it also includes a quantifiable number of cases.

ABOUT PREPOSITIONS

Despite the emphasis in this book on systematic thinking and logic, when it comes to pairing English prepositions with other words, there is little logic. The choice of what preposition to use is often confusing. Prepositions can be especially difficult for non native English speakers because the rules governing prepositions range from vague to nonexistent.

Prepositions, however, show relationships between ideas and need to be taken seriously. For example:

> Internal auditors were recruited *from* over 50 different countries and worked *in* many different locations.

Now, by alternating the prepositions, the meaning changes entirely:

> Internal auditors were recruited in over 50 different countries and worked from many different locations.

Just because prepositions are short does not mean their effects will not be longstanding.

Here are a few frequently misused or confused prepositions:

- *Among* applies to more than two; among friends.
- *Between* is used when only two are involved; between you and me (not myself!).
- *About* can be used as an adjective meaning approximate (a better word to use in reports) but can also be a preposition as in: They wrote about security issues.
- *Beside* means at the side of, *besides* means in addition to.

Because the word "agree" is used so frequently among auditors, and because the question of which preposition, if any, to use with "agree" can be a "sticky wicket,"[3] additional information about that popular word seems in order. From one of the most august and authoritative sources, Fowler's *Modern English Usage*, comes the following:

> The normal uses of agree are as an intransitive verb with a preposition, e.g., agree with, concur with, a person; agree to, consent to a project; agree on, decide something by mutual consent. Its use as a transitive verb...without "on," was said...to be applicable only to discrepant accounts and the like, but it is now much more widely used.[4]

You can say that again!

For example, the following do not require any preposition:

> An agreed statement was issued after the meeting.

> The committee has power to agree its own procedure.

For the record, the usual preposition combinations with "agree" are:

- *Agree to*: Do you agree to this proposal?
- *Agree on*: The Audit Committee agreed on revenue recognition procedures.
- *Agree with*: The auditor agreed with the systems programmer on security controls.

A few more tips on verb/preposition combinations:

- *Correspond to* means match up, tally.
- *Correspond with* means exchange emails or be in agreement with.
- *Compare to* means to liken to something; Shall I compare thee to a summer's day?
- *Compare with* implies doing more work and evaluation.
- *Connect to* applies to things; *connect with*, to people.
- *Different from* is American style, *different to* is British usage.
- *Report on* and *report of* are often used interchangeably. However, a lengthy listing of specific controls that failed tends to be a report on operational discrepancies. And a few emphatic words can be a report of material discrepancies!

This chapter ends with a few sample sentences, wilted by wandering modifiers and ambiguous phrases. Livelier examples, improved by restructuring and editing, follow.

Samples in need of improvement:

1. Findings are presented either as proposed adjustments or reclassifications together with other balance sheet and internal control issues along with management comments which describe their proposed action plan.
2. In planning and performing our audit of the financial statements of ABC Company as of and for the year ended December 31, 20XX, in accordance with auditing standards generally accepted in the United States of America, we considered ABC Company's internal control over financial reporting (internal control) as a basis for designing our auditing procedures for the purpose of expressing our opinion on the financial statements, but not for the purpose of expressing an opinion on the effectiveness of the Company's internal control.
3. The current Q3 balance of USD 50 million is USD 25 million lower than last quarter as expected.

4. The requirement for CEOs and CFOs to certify and attest to the company's financial statements can result in the audit committee being more involved with management and it could also raise issues with respect to management believing that the Board and Audit Committee are too involved and second-guessing management.

5. The steps involved in IT security policies as well as change management processes are important for auditors to be aware of.

Corrected versions:

1. Findings are presented either as proposed adjustments or reclassifications. Management comments, which describe their proposed action plan, and other balance sheet and internal control issues are also presented.

2. XYZ Firm audited the financial statements of ABC Company for the year ended December 31, 20XX, in accordance with auditing standards generally accepted in the United States. We considered ABC Company's internal control over financial reporting (internal control) as a basis for designing our auditing procedures and expressing our opinion on the financial statements, not to express an opinion on the effectiveness of the Company's internal control.

3. As expected, the Q3 balance of USD 50 million is USD 25 million lower than the Q2 balance.

4. The requirement for CEOs and CFOs to certify the company's financial statements can result in greater Audit Committee involvement with management. This requirement could also raise concerns that the Board and Audit Committee might become too involved and engage in "second-guessing" management.

5. Auditors must be aware of the steps involved in IT security policies, as well as change management processes.

Notes

1. PCAOB By-Laws and Standards, Amendment to AU Sec. 543, *Part of Audit Performed by Other Independent Auditors.*
2. Eric Wensberg, *Modern American Usage: A Guide by Wilson Follett* (New York: Hill & Wang, 1998).
3. Robert L. Chapman, Ph.D., *American Slang* (New York: Harper-Collins, 1998). "Sticky wicket" refers to a very difficult or awkward situation and is a term borrowed from the English game of cricket.
4. H.W. Fowler, *Modern English Usage,* 2nd ed. (New York and Oxford: Oxford University Press, 1967).

CHAPTER 8

PARAGRAPHS, PUNCTUATION, AND CAPITALIZATION

Without paragraphs, punctuation, and capitalization, writing would go on and on, spewing information without providing anything particular to focus on. We've all been subjected to presentations like that. In fact, in *Beyond Bullet Points*, Cliff Atkinson makes the powerful point that applying story structure to business presentations takes them beyond boring lists of data and makes them focused and engaging.[1] Story structure also works for written presentations—that is, reports. The topic sentences and transition words of paragraphs and the visual markers of punctuation and capitalization are all tools that help make that structure evident.

The whole point of punctuation is to clarify understanding in the absence of pauses, facial gestures, intonation, and other body English. Words alone are not enough to convey meaning, particularly when the subject matter is complex.

Even basic messages can be turned upside-down when they are punctuated differently. The following letters contain the same words, but the punctuation and capitalization—and meanings—are different.

Dear John,

I want a man who knows what love is all about. You are generous, kind, thoughtful. People who are not like you admit to being inferior. You have ruined me for other men. I yearn for you! I have no feelings whatsoever when we're apart. I can be forever happy—will you let me be yours?

Maria

Dear John,

I want a man who knows what love is. All about you are generous, kind, thoughtful people, who are not like you. Admit to being inferior! You have ruined me. For other men, I yearn. For you, I have no feelings whatsoever. When we're apart, I can be forever happy. Will you let me be?

Yours,

Maria

Undifferentiated audit writing might look like this:

depreciation is calculated on assets more than 90 days in suspense by taking the balance of all suspense accounts and assuming the assets to have a life of five years per internal audits review the spreadsheet used to calculate the figure had the following errors it did not take into account assets between 90 and 120 days and instead started from 120 to 150 days as the first month of depreciation each suspense clearing account had numerous mismatched credits which were not part of . . .

You get the message.

This chapter will demonstrate best practices for composing paragraphs that logically tell the story and for using punctuation to further clarify its meaning.

PARAGRAPH GUIDELINES

Without visual elements that draw attention to certain words and clue in readers about when to pause or stop, writing becomes an obstacle to communication instead of a medium of information. Paragraphs are one of the elements that give messages a chance to be seen as separate and give readers a clearer sense of what is related information. Surrounding important messages with white space and supplying liberal paragraph breaks is as effective as punctuating conversation with moments of silence. Empty areas on a page are *not* wasted.

Like sentences, paragraphs should also be coherent—and as short as possible. And yes, it's okay to have a one-sentence paragraph.

Anyone who has received e-mails that contain no paragraph breaks knows how tedious it is to read unbroken text. Breaks—and brakes!—are needed to stop the reader and announce the beginning of something different from what has been said so far. To make paragraphs work to your advantage, keep them coherent. That means, keep related ideas close to each other, in priority order.

Coherent writing, more than any other quality, will convince the people who read your report that you know what you are talking about. Anybody can generate a list of facts (that job is being delegated to computers anyway), but it takes HOTS (described in Chapter 1) to synthesize disparate data into compelling conclusions.

With tabular formats, paragraph structure requires different considerations. Although the space is predefined, it is crucial that the thoughts tie together. Even though tables contain and often limit the number of words, the rules of coherence do not permit dumping a list of unrelated facts. Well-structured paragraphs start with *topic sentences*, which serve as billboards for what the paragraph is about. Then *transition words* link the related ideas. Each paragraph thus becomes a coherent chunk of information that can stand alone or be connected to other chunks.

Topic Sentences as Billboards

What's a topic sentence? The one sentence that best articulates what the whole paragraph is about. In business writing, the topic sentence should be the first sentence in the paragraph.

If you could select only one sentence from the following paragraph without changing or rearranging any words, which one best expresses the main idea?

> The chief audit executive should develop and maintain a quality assurance and improvement program that covers all aspects of the internal audit activity and continuously monitors its effectiveness. The program should include periodic and external quality assessments and ongoing internal monitoring. Each part of the program should be designed to help the internal auditing activity add value and improve the organization's operations and to provide assurance that the internal audit activity is in conformity with the *Standards* and the *Code of Ethics*.

Well, it's an easy one. The first sentence best captures the main message and is therefore the topic sentence. In report writing, the first sentence should always capture the message and state the topic.

By being placed first, the topic sentence serves as another useful billboard—like the tables of contents, headings, and subheadings described in Chapter 4. When the message of each paragraph is succinctly stated in the first sentence, skim-it-fast readers (translation: CAEs and Audit Committees) can zoom through reports reading only first sentences—and not miss a thing.

The rule for topic sentences is that they should accurately describe what follows—no less, no more. For instance, if high-level risks are declared the topic in the first sentence, that paragraph should exclude data related to medium- or low-level risk. Conversely, if management's response to all identified risks is the topic, then all levels should be included.

The communication principle behind topic sentences is related to the journalism axiom: Don't bury the lead. Too often, highly intelligent, logical writers, who know the subject inside out, start paragraphs or sections of a document by stating background and setting the scene for a major pronouncement—only to have that pronouncement buried within the details and lose its impact. In English, what is stated first is considered most important. So start with the main point. Cut to the chase. Forget the wind-up; make the pitch.

Smooth Transitions

Transition words are the secret weapon wielded by strong business writers. They seem so unimpressive when listed on a page: *then, next, at first,* and so on. But used effectively, they can clarify even the most complex message.

Here is a chart of transition words that might be useful in audit reports:

To add ideas together	*To give examples or emphasis*
and	for example
also	specifically
moreover	in particular
in addition	that is
further	in fact
first, second	most important
then	indeed
next, finally	above all
equally important	

To show time	*To summarize*
soon	therefore
after	consequently
previously	as a result
meanwhile	in conclusion, to conclude
before	

To make contrasts
nevertheless
in contrast
however
but
instead

And here is a paragraph that could use some smooth transitions.

The auditors hold an entrance conference. This is to provide the management officials responsible for the function or activity being reviewed with a description of the audit scope and objectives. Time frames for completing the audit; access to required records, information and personnel; and introduction of the audit team members are usually covered. Management usually designates a convenient working area for audit staff and an audit liaison official for audit matters. The audit team considers management's suggestions on additional areas to include in the audit, as well as identification of potential areas which may warrant special review.

It's one thing to cut to the chase, but when a series of conditions, actions, or events is being communicated, it helps to establish a starting point. The revised version not only includes transitions, but it also prepares readers for what is coming and, when the end is reached, they know they have arrived.

At the beginning of each audit, the auditors hold an entrance conference. The purpose is to provide management officials responsible for the function or activity being reviewed with a description of the audit scope and objectives. Other areas usually covered include: time frames for completing the audit; access to required records, information and personnel; and introduction of the audit team members. Normally, management designates a convenient working area for audit staff and an audit liaison official for audit matters. In addition, the audit team considers management's suggestions on areas to include in the audit and the identification of potential risk areas which may warrant special review.

PUNCTUATION MATTERS

Punctuation matters. All those little symbols are necessary to replace the gestures and intonation we use when we speak to someone. In the absence of such body language, punctuation is needed for written words to ensure that thoughts are presented in ways that will not be misinterpreted. Even small commas can make big differences.

Consider these two sentences:

The Democrats say the Republicans will win the election.

The Democrats, say the Republicans, will win the election.

The addition of only two commas has shifted the meaning entirely. An unlikely statement in both instances, yes, but the impact of that small elliptical shape is enormous. Be careful where you put them in your reports.

And forget the rule about always using a comma before the word "and." Only when the "and" clause is independent (i.e., names its own subject and predicate) is the comma needed.

For example, here are two versions of the same thought:

> We would like to request a product presentation from our software vendors, and they will be invited to participate in an in-house evaluation.

The comma before "and" is needed in this version because "they will be invited to participate in an in-house evaluation" can stand alone as a complete thought; it could, in fact, be a separate sentence. This next version, however, has only one independent clause:

> We would like to request a product presentation from our software vendors and will invite them to participate in an in-house evaluation.

The comma is not appropriate here because "will invite them to participate" names no subject and is therefore a dependent clause. Ahem, no comma before "and is therefore a dependent clause" either.

Margaret Schertzer's handy *Elements of Grammar* contains accessible, practical information about many grammatical details, and her section on punctuation includes periods, quotation marks, exclamation points, question marks, and ellipsis dots,[2] but here are selected punctuation rules that will be most useful in internal audit reporting.

Apostrophe

Apostrophes are used to show possession, to indicate omitted letters in contractions, and to indicate plurals when the addition of "s" would be confusing.

Joe's report, Joe and Mary's report, Joe's and Mary's reports

don't, shouldn't

Oakland A's

Note that "it's" is *not* possessive—it's the most commonly mistaken exception to the possessive rule. *It's* means "it is;" *its*, with no apostrophe, is possessive.

"It's on its way" (meaning the report, of course) is a quick way to keep them straight.

Colon

Colons are used to precede lists, formal quotations, and bullet points.

> Company locations include: England, India, China, Indonesia, and Japan.

> In response to the findings, Financial Controller J. Smith said: "xxxxx."

> We noted the following in our review:

> -
> -
> -

> (no punctuation is required following bullet points unless each item is a complete sentence)

Colons were formerly used after the salutation of a letter, but most business writers use commas these days. For example: Dear Mr. Gates,

Comma

Commas are the most frequently used—and misused—punctuation mark.

They are used in business writing to:

1. Set off nonrestrictive appositives:

   The meeting, which was attended by the Chief Audit Executive and Audit Committee Chair, was preceded by a seminar on Sarbanes-Oxley Section 404.

2. Join independent clauses:

   A sequential invoicing system will not offer more significant benefits than the current one, and we will review the current system in the third quarter.

3. Separate consecutive adjectives or items in a series:

Internal Audit reviewed and tested samples of: Purchases, Accounts Payable and Accrued Expenses, Revenue and Receivables, Computer Security, and Customs Documentation.

4. Set off contrasting phrases:

Four transfers were not supported by a signed authorization, three were supported in detail.

5. Follow introductory clauses:

Because of complicated logistics and inadequate banking facilities at the border, it is not possible to make funds available to the Customs Department in time.

6. Set off dates:

By February 19, 2007, we need a list of all items with a sales value greater than USD 1000 that are exempted from the 2% freight calculation.

7. Separate words or numbers where omission of the comma could cause confusion:

Of this amount, USD 102,339 was deferred over 720 days; USD 57,995, over 180 days; and USD 207,178, over 120 days.

Semicolon

Semicolons are used:

1. Between closely related independent clauses:

No payments over USD 150 should be made from petty cash; and entertainment expenses should be approved via Purchase Order.

2. When you want a break stronger than a comma but not as strong as a period:

Service reports are not prenumbered; however, they are controlled by job number and date.

3. In sentences with an abundance of commas:

Reports dated January 15, 2007; February 17, 2007; and March 10, 2007 were filed without job numbers.

Hyphen

Hyphens are used to link certain letters, numbers, or words to prevent ambiguity and confusion—and to divide words at the right page margin; the dictionary shows correct syllable division.

> long-term investment
>
> five-year maturity
>
> year-end

Where the same word can be a noun or a verb, generally the noun is hyphenated.

For example:

> Follow-up is a noun, follow up is a verb
>
> Write-off is a noun, write off is a verb

CAPITAL RULES

Capitalization is another visual detail that can reinforce or undermine credibility. Just as number variances are scrutinized, three different ways of referring to the same entity can cause confusion and raise doubts about other components of the report. For example:

> The IIA Standards of Professional Practice
> The IIA standards of professional practice
> The IIA Standards of professional practice

Consistent capitalization not only looks better, it also promotes confidence that the information in the report is trustworthy.

Many companies have established their own style guides that dictate what to capitalize, but the general categories that should always be capitalized are:

- The first word of every sentence
- Proper nouns (i.e., the names of specific people, organizations, companies, countries)

- Titles—of people, reports, auditing standards, report categories
- Days of the week, months of the year

In one of its earlier editions, *The New York Times Manual of Style and Usage* noted that "there is little difference between a Martini and a martini, but a rule can shield against untidiness in detail that might make readers doubt large facts."[3] Let's drink to that. And incorporate the keen observation of details like these into the final stages of the report-writing process. Editing—and graphics—are the subjects of Chapter 9.

Notes

1. Cliff Atkinson, *Beyond Bullet Points* (Redmond, WA: Microsoft Press, 2005).
2. Margaret Schertzer, *The Elements of Grammar* (New York: MacMillan, 1986).
3. Allan M. Siegal and William G. Connolly, *The New York Times Manual of Style and Usage* (New York: The New York Times Company, 1999).

GRAPHICS AND EDITING

Transforming raw data into information and translating that information into actionable messages is a demanding task. As in any kind of communication, a visual is worth a thousand words; and in the case of audit reports, maybe a million dollars. Therefore, this chapter will provide tips on how to best incorporate graphic elements into the internal audit reporting process.

As that process reaches its conclusion, editing is essential. To edit does not mean merely to shorten the text or just correct the misspellings that the spellcheck software caught. As a critical component of the audit reporting process, the edit is the comprehensive, big-picture examination of the document that gives the auditors one more chance to make sure the headings match the ones in the Table of Contents, to count the pieces, and to produce a precision report. Tips and Techniques on how to mentally achieve enough objectivity to edit successfully are also offered in this chapter.

MAKING REPORTS LOOK GOOD

Auditors should consider graphics as part of the report-writing process for two reasons: (1) drawing attention to certain findings and recommendations is required to make a convincing case; and (2) people are more inclined to read material that is attractively presented. It's that simple.

Paragraph breaks, headings, and other billboard devices were discussed in previous chapters. Here, the more formal graphic elements, such as tables and graphs, will be considered.

A comprehensive look at graphic design is beyond the scope of this book, but the most important principles will be reviewed. For more information and examples of graphic excellence, the books written by Edward R. Tufte and Stephen Few are recommended, and some are listed in the Bibliography, Appendix C.

The short list of best practices regarding MS Excel tables and other software graphics tools internal auditors are most apt to use reads as follows:

1. Spell out any terms that may be unknown to anyone using the report.
2. Insert words horizontally only.
3. Use consistent spacing and minimal special effects.
4. Proofread at least once.
5. Print a test run or e-mail it to yourself to see how it translates.

"Any design method that works effectively without drawing attention away from the data is invaluable," says Stephen Few, and he emphasizes the value of white space. If rows of data are too close together, they are difficult to read and comprehend, and he points out that white space can be manipulated to direct readers to scan either horizontally or vertically by varying the amount of white space between either the rows or the columns.[1]

TABLES, FOOTNOTES, AND GRAPHS

Tables

Here are four factoids regarding tables:

1. Tables are useful for showing large numbers of specific, related facts or statistics in a small space.

2. Tables should be numbered, using Arabic numerals, in the order they appear in the text. Then refer to "Table 1" rather than "the table below."

3. The title or caption, above the body of the table, briefly identifies the table. Use this title consistently throughout the document—same exact words. It may seem like a small point, but calling a data set "Transaction fees and costs" on one page and "Fees and other acquisition costs" on another gives readers free-floating doubts that can undermine credibility. Reports, and especially tables, are not the place to exhibit vocabulary versatility. If writers get tired of using the same terms, they should use them anyway (another phrase comes to mind, but I figured my editor might object). But back to the table at hand.

4. The boxhead carries the column headings, which should be concise but descriptive. Avoid vertical lettering.

Footnotes

Tables often require further explanation, thus the practicality of footnotes.

Here are three techniques for showing footnotes:

1. Footnotes are normally set one size smaller than the body of a table.

2. Numbers should not be used to identify footnotes in a table because they may be mistaken for the data.

3. Footnotes generally comprise four types and should appear as follows:

   1. Source notes (marked *Sources*)
   2. General notes (marked *Notes*)
   3. Notes on specific parts of the table (use "a," then "b," etc.; the series starts over for each table)
   4. Notes on level of probability (use asterisks)

Graphs

Graphs represent numerical data in visual form and are especially useful for showing trends, movements, distributions, and cycles. Graphs can show a visual significance in the data that is not readily apparent in text; however, they are not as accurate as tables. The two most common graphs are line graphs and bar graphs:

- *Line graphs* show the relationship between two sets of numbers.
- *Bar graphs* are generally used to show quantities of:
  - The same item at different times
  - Different items at the same time
  - Different parts of an item that make up the whole

The idea is to select graphs that accurately present data in its simplest form so the significance can be grasped with the least amount of effort or visual distraction.

Edward Tufte says: "Graphic excellence is that which gives to the viewer the greatest number of ideas in the shortest time with the least ink in the smallest space." He also says: "Graphical displays should be closely integrated with the statistical and verbal descriptions of a data set."[2]

Therefore, the incorporation of tables and charts into an audit report must be done with planning. Displaying a table with no explanation of the implications of the data is rarely sufficient. Furthermore, internal audit reports are written to provide "illustration of a settled finding,"[3]

GRAPHICS TIPS AND TECHNIQUES

Best uses of various graphic elements:

- *Tables*—to compare data
- *Line graphs*—to show changes over time
- *Bar graphs*—to compare data and emphasize differences

(continued)

GRAPHICS TIPS AND TECHNIQUES *(continued)*

- *Photographs and video*—to show physical conditions
- *Pie charts*—to show proportional distributions in data

Best practices techniques:

- Make the graphics *horizontal*
- *Spell out words* and avoid mysterious coding
- Run *graphics into the text* whenever possible
- Use clear, consistent *labeling*
- Write out *critical implications*—of the data

---

in Tufte's words. And any explanatory text should tell the reader what to read, not how to read it.

ANOTHER LOOK AT REPORTS

Taking a second look at any audit report to be sure that names and titles are spelled correctly, that dates and all other numbers are accurate, that headings and subheadings match the table of contents, and that tables are identified properly is essential. That second look is called editing.

Before beginning an edit, know that automated spellcheckers are not infallible. While the little red lines generated by most of the available software do alert writers to many misspellings, correctly spelled but incorrectly chosen words routinely slip through. Here are just a few common escapees:

- T/he
- Filed/field
- Verbs meant to be past tense that end in e, such as measure/d, note/d

Then, once the red-line fields have been successfully crossed, here are ten things to do to ensure that what you meant to say was actually said.

TEN EDITING TIPS AND TECHNIQUES

1. Count the pieces and check the layout.
2. Look for –ion and –ment words.
3. Delete adverbs and other unnecessary words.
4. Mentally remove the words between the commas.
5. Make sure subjects and verbs agree in number.
6. Relocate misplaced modifiers.
7. Use an active, personal sentence structure.
8. Check for topic sentences.
9. Read it backward.
10. Read it aloud—and have someone else read it.

Counting the Pieces

Counting the pieces is a less formal way of referring to graphic continuity. Make sure the items referenced in the Table of Contents exist in the same order in which they are listed—and that each of the terms is spelled the same and that tables or exhibits are titled the same. Though it may seem like a simple thing, naming the same categories different things can cause confusion when the original writers are not available to explain, and why spend time explaining simple things when more material issues need to be discussed? Along with checking content consistency, make sure the layout does not contain holes or a series of capital letters that spell trouble. Graphic continuity is a high-paying job in the movie business because continuity matters.

–ion and –ment Words

Those multisyllable -ion and -ment words are the verbs made into nouns covered in Chapter 6. Replace any tedious, boring bureaucrat-ese with active, vibrant, easy-to-see words.

Avoid Adverbs

Adverbs, the words that editorially comment on how something is done, should be avoided. One person's "quickly" is another person's "timely," and no reader really knows what either term means. Look for any words ending in -ly, and delete most of them. Also delete any other words that do not contribute specificity to the message.

Between the Commas

Mentally removing the words between the commas is a good check on what you are, in fact, saying. When "in fact" is removed from that sentence, the idea that "removing . . . is a good check on what you are . . . saying" is clear. By reading selected sentences (usually the longer ones) and isolating the words before and after the commas, you can check the logic as well as the punctuation. At this point, also check for periods, hyphens, and other necessary punctuation.

Subject/Verb

As you review the punctuation, also check to be sure that subjects and verbs agree in number. Plural subjects separated from the verbs by lengthy qualifying phrases, particularly when the commas were omitted, are easiest to spot; singular subjects are hardest.

Misplaced Modifiers

At the same time you scan those qualifying phrases, you can review for misplaced modifiers. Are the descriptive phrases in the right place in the sentence? Not stuffing any employees into the drawer are you? Good.

Keep Active

Active sentence structure is another item to check while you are scanning. (The good thing about these editing tips is that you can multitask them). Most software will pick up the passive constructions, so pay attention to those green lines as well as the red ones.

Lead with the Topic

Now check that each paragraph starts with a topic sentence. I know, you might have to create a category to describe what some paragraphs are about, but as you read back through, scan only the first sentence of each paragraph, and you should see the big picture.

The next two techniques involve going over the material in a different way than the usual rushed and silent read-through. They allow you to distance yourself from the material sufficiently to pick up things that your writer/auditor's mind might simply accept because of the familiarity of the subject—but that readers might find confusing.

Reading Backward

Reading the text backward allows you to let go of the meaning long enough to notice the form. It is especially useful for spotting typos and unnecessary words.

Reading Aloud

Saying words aloud will *always* reveal weaknesses of syntax. Of course, an objective third-party read is best, and presents an excellent opportunity to practice those collaboration skills. Hey, promise that you will read their report next time. Internal audit reporting is not a solitary profession.

Notes

1. Stephen Few, *Show Me the Numbers* (Oakland, CA: Analytics Press, 2004).
2. Edward Tufte, *The Visual Display of Quantitative Information* (Cheshire, CT: Graphics Press, 1983).
3. Ibid.

IT'S A FLAT WORLD
AFTER ALL

For all information's independence and extent, it is people, in their communities, organizations, and institutions, who ultimately decide what it all means and why it matters.

John Seely Brown and Paul Duguid,
The Social Life of Information

This section comprises only one chapter and is composed of five parts. The first part observes the SOX effect on internal auditing processes around the world and offers a rationale for why this particular legislation is reaching far beyond the companies that are legally bound by it.

The second part deals with diversity: how to measure cultural commonalities and get the job done in a variety of settings. Audience analysis checklists and advice from experts on how best to report to multinational audiences are included.

The third part addresses the question "Why English?" and provides a few pointers on particular pitfalls to be aware of, plus notes for reporting in multiple currencies.

The fourth part offers suggestions for getting past writer's block and getting started, and the fifth part offers a few last words in support of an internal audit reporting process that is becoming increasingly more important, more automated, and decidedly global.

PERSPECTIVE

Ted Senko, Global Leader of Internal Audit Services, KPMG, says: "With respect to the whole Internal Audit profession, SOX has enlarged the view from within organizations—and from without. Internal Audit now has the opportunity to operate at a level they've never operated at before—and everybody gets it. There is wide proliferation of SOX-inspired standards in Europe, Asia, Australia, and South America; companies are modeling the best of what has been learned in the U.S. in order to improve corporate governance through process advancements and quality controls. With a strong understanding of processes and risk identification as core competencies, Internal Audit can be the eyes and ears, an early warning system, a vital link between board and management."

CHAPTER 10

IT'S A FLAT WORLD
AFTER ALL

PART ONE: THE LONG REACH OF SOX

SOX requirements are paving the way for an expansion of the role of the internal auditor, both within individual companies and around the world. Some multinationals have already been complying with SOX requirements, even before being legally bound to do so. Banking organizations have been using the COSO framework and Section 404 too, as have healthcare and other not-for-profit organizations. According to feedback posted by the PCAOB/SEC, following a roundtable held on May 10, 2006, many financial executives believe that incorporating the spirit—and in many cases, the letter—of SOX leads to better-managed businesses and, consequently, more profitable and sustainable ones.[1]

At the same time, the costs of SOX compliance have been the subject of lengthy debates ever since the legislation was passed. Why then might so many companies choose to comply with this legislation? "Even in countries where audit reporting is not governed by SOX, many executives are voluntarily complying with its requirements," said a General Manager with SAP. "They feel that with better controls in place, their reporting will be more credible, customers and investors will have more confidence, and they will achieve a premium place in the market."[2]

How the SOX legislation will be specifically implemented and to what degree it will apply to smaller companies are yet to be fully determined.

However, the process of collaborative communication in which the details are worked out is valuable in itself.

A Houston hospital CFO said:

> While non-profit and governmental organizations are not held to the same standards as publicly-traded companies, many provisions of Sarbanes-Oxley constitute sound ethical and business practices. In fact, its adoption is a valuable tool to help educate and engage the CEO and Board in implementing more disciplined approaches to their fiduciary responsibilities.[3]

Indeed. The basic goals of SOX—accountability, connecting conditions to consequences, and improved internal controls—are beneficial for any business.

PART TWO: ANALYZING AUDIENCES

Diversity is a good thing; if we were all alike, the species would die out. But diversity also brings confusion and chaos at times—and thus requires effective communication skills. And as diversity increases, those skills need to be cranked up a notch. Language can often be a barrier instead of a bridge. That is why it is so important to first observe, analyze, and listen. Then begin to communicate.

One listing of how-tos with respect to Asia-Pacific communications includes the following suggestions: set up personal meetings and lay foundations that will demonstrate your reliability, be clear and concise, avoid surprises, follow up promptly and precisely, and don't be a phony.[4] That's good advice for doing business in any unfamiliar (the word "foreign" sometimes implies strange or incomprehensible) cultural milieu.

Even before taking those steps, it's a good idea to mentally review the new situation and proactively analyze the differences—and similarities—of the organization being audited and the corporate culture in which it operates.

One analytical tool to help make that comparison is the Global Integrator, developed by The Swiss Consulting Group. The Global Integrator is a graph that visually plots points of cultural commonality—and points where attitudes and habits differ (see Exhibit 10.1).

EXHIBIT 10.1 *The Global Integrator*

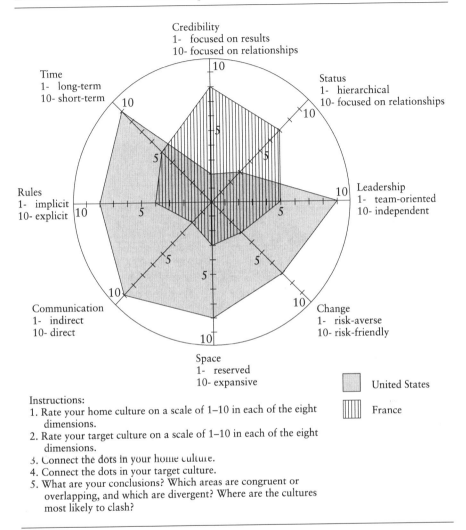

Instructions:
1. Rate your home culture on a scale of 1–10 in each of the eight dimensions.
2. Rate your target culture on a scale of 1–10 in each of the eight dimensions.
3. Connect the dots in your home culture.
4. Connect the dots in your target culture.
5. What are your conclusions? Which areas are congruent or overlapping, and which are divergent? Where are the cultures most likely to clash?

Note: By way of illustration, this sample compares the United States and France. All dimensions and ratings are generalizations and only approximate reality.[5] Reprinted by permission from Thomas D. Zweifel, *Culture Clash*.

The Global Integrator focuses on eight categories for cultural comparison: credibility, status, leadership, change, space, communication, rules, and time. In order to arrive at the ratings, questions in each category need to be carefully developed. For instance, in the area of communication, some of the questions might be: What medium works best—e-mail or voice messages? How should I respond to silence in this culture? What do I say if I have made an error?

With respect to internal audit reporting, some of the questions to consider might be: Are current IIA standards being followed? What other auditing regulations are significant here? Which IT software is in place? Should agenda items for the audit planning meeting be approved in advance?

Taking time to evaluate how one set of values meshes with another can smooth the audit reporting process and make communicating the engagement results much easier.

Analyzing Specific Audiences

While the Global Integrator provides a big-picture analysis in cultural terms, specific questions about each audit need to be answered as well.

A prereport, audience analysis checklist might go something like this:

- *What are the names and titles of the recipients?* And what information do they need to know? If you do not know who the recipients are, find out. No written document can be effective unless it is directed to specific recipients.
- *What are the primary areas of concern?* Internal auditors know what the essential findings and recommendations are, but it helps to look at them from the audience's point of view.
- *Are the report recipients new to the company or the committee?* Are they experts? Do they think they are experts? The last group is hardest to write for, but sufficient appendices, charts, and tables can reassure even the most skeptical reader. Some people want more detail, while some prefer the big picture. Some simply want to know only what is different—or what they have missed.

Listening around the World

After thoughtful analysis of the group, the next step is to listen to the individuals within it. Listening is one of the least appreciated business communication skills, and yet is one of the most valuable. A quick test for effective listening was supplied in Chapter 1, but the best way to become a better listener is to tune in to what others are saying. Really tune in.

According to international consultant Thomas Zweifel, the levels of listening progress from "pretending to listen" all the way up to "mastery," which is the ability to hear how our own words are being received. He notes that: "The Chinese word for *listening* also means *eyes, ears, you, undivided attention,* and *love.*" And he says: "The practice of listening consistent with these rich meanings may well be one of the most important leverage points in shaping your company's future. To say it bluntly: Shut up and listen for a change."[6]

An international anecdote about listening that Dr. Zweifel tells, which bears repeating, refers to a meeting between Gore Vidal and Henry Kissinger in Rome. Mr. Vidal says: "Although Kissinger and I were careful to keep some distance apart, I could hear the ceaseless rumbling voice in every corner of the chapel. The German accent is more pronounced in Europe than on television at home. He has a brother who came to America when he did. Recently the brother was asked why he had no German accent but Henry did. 'Because,' said the brother, 'Henry never listens.'" [7]

Effective Reporting around the World

After the observation, the analysis, and the listening comes effective reporting. What should internal auditors working in multinational organizations do differently? Are there particular communication biases regarding international audit reporting?

Stephane Girard's advice to multinational auditors is no different than for domestic ones:

> Number one, be effective by identifying and auditing controls over key risks for the corporation and by communicating the audit result in a loud and clear manner. Effective identification and auditing requires risk-based audit plans for every engagement; effective communication requires short reports that link the findings to the risks and propose practical recommendations. Number two, be efficient in optimizing audit time by using IT to "industrialize" report generation—and by not focusing on minor risk.[8]

One Senior IT Auditor interacts with about a dozen overseas locations that each have different software. He says the first thing auditors need to do is talk to the local financial controller or country manager to determine the software inventory. The next task is to look at the different processes—such as change management, new hires, security policies—and become familiar with the steps involved in each. Then, the controls that relate to those processes must be developed and designed using the COBIT/COSO or ITIL. "At this stage we do the risk analysis and identify the key or primary controls based on risk to financial impact on the company," he says. "When appropriate controls are set up, it is important that the external auditors 'buy in'—then the actual testing and fieldwork can begin."

The final step is production of either an operational or a design deficiency report that includes controls that failed, management's response, the remediation date for retesting, and any further potential risks. And in terms of cross-cultural people skills, he says: "Don't force the process. Find out what theirs is—and be willing to modify any preconceived ideas about what will work."[9]

Irv Diamond has served on numerous audit committees for companies of all sizes, both public and private. He says one of the biggest challenges for internal auditors reporting in a global context is to understand what each committee needs with respect to unique, local attitudes about internal control and documentation. "Don't make assumptions," he says, "especially about inventories—which are often tough—reserves, and values of fixed assets." He recommends hiring internal auditors who understand the local accounting mores and who know the territory. But, he says, "no matter where internal auditors are located, the most important reporting consideration is to concentrate on critical issues and get to the bottom line right at the beginning."[10]

And another Corporate Board Member and Audit Committee Chair advises multinational internal auditors to conform to Generally Accepted Accounting Principles (GAAP), to be aware of the Foreign Corrupt Practices Act, and to adhere to the requirements of Section 404 of SOX. "Internal Auditors play a very important role as they are the first line of defense," he said. "Learning new perspectives is no longer just a nice thing to do, it is required."[11]

PART THREE: WHY ENGLISH?

Estimates vary, but English is generally considered to be the second most widely spoken language in the world, with from 460 to 514 million speakers, after Mandarin.[12] Furthermore, it is estimated that more than 80 percent of the homepages on the Web are in English, while the next highest percentages are 4.5 percent for German and 3.1 percent for Japanese.[13]

Is it because English has the most available words to use that it is so widely used? Some estimates say so, but perhaps the influence of computers and world trade have proliferated English.

The English language is extremely inconsistent regarding usage, pronunciation, and spelling. There are almost as many exceptions as rules. But it offers a flexibility that many languages do not have: the immediate acceptance of foreign and/or new words. New terms, and thus new concepts, can be incorporated simply by importing them, with no translation needed. These terms are soon established in the language and appear in the dictionaries, for example: *faux pas, perestroika, fajita, ad hoc, per capita,* and many more.

This instant vocabulary expansion also allows for the spontaneous addition of new ideas and new ways of doing things. Technology has contributed a significant body of new words: *podcast, reboot, search engine, scalable, smiley*—or *emoticon*—to name a few. In *Information Anxiety*, Richard Saul Wurman says: "When you learn a new language, you are not just learning a new vocabulary and grammar, but a new, or at least a slightly different, way of thinking."[14]

Another note is in order regarding the differences between American English and British English. This book uses the former, which, although a descendant of the latter, often applies different meanings to the same words. For example, a rubber in the UK is an eraser. People educated in India or other countries influenced by the original British English may find some of the information in this book inconsistent with what they were taught.

Particular Pitfalls

The idioms, idiosyncrasies, and peculiarities inherent in English can make it challenging to learn. For example, "effect" is both a verb and a noun, and recently "impact" has joined the club. Not to mention the host of other homonyms, words spelled alike but having different meanings and pronunciations. As in: The bandage was *wound* around the *wound.*

And in what other language do people recite at a play and play at a recital? Ship by truck and send cargo by ship? And how can a slim chance and a fat chance be the same, while a wise man and a wise guy are opposites? A house can burn up as it burns down, you fill in a form by filling it out, and an alarm goes off by going on.

There are no masculine and feminine words to worry about in English, but the irregularity of so many of the verbs (e.g., go, went, gone) makes up for that simplification. Also, singular verb forms often end with an "s"—the usual designation for plurals: The auditor reports, the auditors report.

When to use the articles "a" or "the" presents problems for non-native speakers because there are no distinct rules. Reading well-written publications is one way to learn those subtle distinctions.

Then, there are the many similar words that confuse even native speakers, such as: *accede* (to agree) and *exceed* (to surpass); *appraise* (to evaluate) and *apprise* (to inform); *infer* (deduce from) and *imply* (indirectly suggest); and *balance* (difference between the debit and credit sides of an account) and *remainder* (the part left over). Not to mention *cite* (to summon to appear in court or quote as an authority), *site* (a location), and *sight* (a view).

Add in the irregular comparative forms of adjectives (e.g., good, better, best), and it becomes impressive to hear people from around the world writing reports and giving presentations in English. Mazeltov!

Multiple Currencies

Reporting accurately in one currency is challenging, but reporting in multiple currencies requires the skills of an accountant! An observant internal auditor should have no trouble dealing with the multiplicity of currencies likely to be encountered in today's flat world.[15]

The trend is toward simplifying the way monetary amounts are written. The symbols for dollar and pound are no longer widely used; most companies opt to use the country code, USD for example, followed by the numeric amount.

With respect to internal audit reports, the most important thing is to be consistent in the way the numbers are shown. For example, if GBP are stated first, followed by USD, that sequence should be followed throughout the report. If tables comparing currency values are used, they should follow the same pattern.

Most newspapers convert monetary amounts to the local currency, at least according to directives from the Associated Press.[16] And it should go without saying that the proper exchange rates need to be used.

PART FOUR: GETTING STARTED

What is commonly referred to as writer's block is in fact thinker's block. Before a thought is fully formed, it is impossible to express it—literally or virtually. However, when the same thought has been processed, expressing it comes naturally.

Sometimes, however, the blockage is physical and, like an otherwise functioning car on a cold morning, the brain simply needs a little warm-up. Here are five ways to rev up your writing engine if it seems to be sluggish:

1. Start moving—the keys, the pen, whatever writing tool you use
2. Start anywhere—at the end, in the middle
3. Program yourself to write at a specific time and place
4. Let it go—get up and move around
5. Say it out loud

Start Moving

Writing is a physical act. You can jumpstart your writing (okay, enough car talk) by simply moving your hands. Let your words come out unedited at this point, because that's what delete buttons are for. Then scan what you see, and, as you correct the obvious glitches, you also give yourself a chance to improve the wording.

Start Anywhere

Start at the end or in the middle. Lose the linear. Linear process works for the audit but is not always best for the writing.

Program Yourself

Tell yourself the day and time when you will write, and your inner computer will be on and ready to proceed efficiently. When you can do your writing in the same location—at a particular desk with a particular computer in a particular light—your mind will be better prepared to produce particularly effective prose. Or, if it's the usual laptop-on-the-plane routine, at least program yourself ahead of time.

Walk Away

Just as moving the keys or the cursor can have a momentum-building effect, getting up and taking a walk also produces results. Getting unstuck mentally sometimes requires a physical change of location. Go outside or down an unfamiliar hallway. Lose yourself. When you return, you will see the information and words differently and you may find solutions that were invisible before.

Say It Out Loud

Listen to yourself say what you have to say. Then key it in or write it down verbatim. You will be surprised how accurate and useable your spoken words are. Writing for the ear usually improves any writing—and gives it power.

PART FIVE: LAST WORDS

Successful media reporters are trained to answer the basic questions in every story, so it is appropriate to address them in this book for front-line financial reporters. The "who and what" of the internal audit function is growing larger, thanks to SOX and automation and a connected world. The following selections from various publications, the PCAOB/SEC roundtable of May 10, 2006, and the IIA focus rather forcefully on "why" internal audit reporting is becoming increasingly important. "How" to follow a specific process and communicate the engagement results more effectively has been discussed and demonstrated in this book. "When?" The bottom line is that the accurate story of global commerce needs to be told now.

> *To prove that it isn't issuing paychecks to fictitious burger-flippers, McDonald's Corp. has turned to specialized software. Like most publicly traded U.S. companies, the fast-food giant has spent much of the past year documenting and testing its "internal controls," or procedures designed to ensure the accuracy of its financial data. This massive effort was triggered by the Sarbanes-Oxley corporate-reform law of 2002. . . .*

The Wall Street Journal, April 25, 2005

> *The Sarbanes-Oxley statute . . . is one of the most influential-and controversial-pieces of corporate legislation ever to have hit a statute book. Its original aim is . . . to improve the accountability of managers to shareholders, and hence to calm the raging crisis of confidence in American capitalism aroused by the scandals at Enron, WorldCom and other companies. The law's . . . implications, for good or ill, are going to be far-reaching. . . .*

The Economist, May 19, 2005

> *Yet many small companies are spending enormous sums looking for signatures and it's hard to convince auditors these signatures are not necessary. They feel a strong need to have documented controls*

whereas I think "tone at the top" is often more analytical in nature. If someone were a lie and a cheat, wouldn't they sign off on the documents anyway?

Robert F. Gallagher, Stratsys, May 10, 2006 PCAOB/SEC Roundtable

As the case against Mr. Lay and Mr. Skilling showed, the laws for corporate conduct are being interpreted strictly, requiring honesty in all actions and statements to avoid prosecution. Failure to be forthright, even in subtle ways, can result in a criminal trial.

The New York Times, May 27, 2006

Walking out of the 2,400-seat ballroom at Tuesday morning's general session, attendees were whispering to each other, "I wish my chief executive officer could hear that speech!" It's no wonder Sy Sternberg, chairman of the board and chief executive officer of New York Life Insurance Co., was greeted with rousing applause for his 90-minute affirmation of internal auditors.

To begin, Sternberg read a letter that he'd received from Houston's now-defunct Enron Corp. It was a letter that Enron sent to all its vendors outlining the company's expectations of them: adherence to Enron's code of ethics and an understanding that Enron may audit the vendor at any time. "This letter," says Sternberg, "reminds me of the wide gulf between the written word and action." In the corporate world, he continued, "a violation of corporate ethics is tantamount to stealing."

The Institute of Internal Auditors, May 20, 2006

Notes

1. Public comments are listed at *www.sec.gov/news/press/4-511.shtml,* and the IIA posted a summary of responses on its Web site as well.
2. Jasvir Gill, General Manager, Governance, Risk and Compliance, SAP, telephone interview, March 2006.
3. Liz Alhand, SVP/CFO, Harris County Hospital District, Texas Medical Center, e-mail correspondence, April 2006.
4. David L. James, *The Executive Guide to Asia-Pacific Communications* (New York: Kodansha International, 1995).

5. Thomas D. Zweifel, Ph.D., *Culture Clash: Managing the Global High Performance Team* (New York: SelectBooks, 2003).
6. Thomas D. Zweifel, Ph.D., *Communicate or Die: Getting Results through Speaking and Listening* (New York: SelectBooks, 2003).
7. Ibid.
8. Stephane Girard, Director of Internal Audit, Schlumberger Ltd., e-mail correspondence, June 2006.
9. Sanjay Gupta, Senior IT Auditor, DIONEX, e-mail correspondence, June 2006.
10. Irv Diamond, Audit Committee Chair, telephone interview, March 2006.
11. William E. Stevens, BBI Group, telephone interview, April 2006.
12. *The New York Times 2006 Almanac,* edited by John W. Wright, (New York: Penguin Group, 2006), supplied the 460 million figure; the *TIME 2006 Almanac,* edited by Borgna Brunner, (Boston: Pearson Education, 2006), supplied the 514 figure.
13. *www.englishenglish.com/english_facts_8.htm.*
14. Richard Saul Wurman, *Information Anxiety* (New York: Doubleday, 1989).
15. Thomas L. Friedman, *The World Is Flat* (New York: Farrar, Strauss, and Giroux, 2005).
16. Norm Goldstein, ed., *The Associated Press Stylebook and Libel Manual,* 6th ed. (New York: The Associated Press, 1996).

APPENDICES

PROFESSIONAL STANDARDS

THE INSTITUTE OF INTERNAL AUDITORS[1]

International Standards for the Professional Practice of Internal Auditing

Selections from the *Introduction,* primarily the changes effective January 2004
Selections from Attribute *Standard 1200*
Performance *Standard 2100* and *Standard 2400*

INTRODUCTION

Internal audit activities are performed in diverse legal and cultural environments; within organizations that vary in purpose, size, complexity, and structure; and by persons within or outside the organization. While differences may affect the practice of internal auditing in each environment, compliance with the International Standards for the Professional Practice of Internal Auditing is essential if the responsibilities of internal

---

[1] From the International Standards for the Professional Practice of Internal Auditing. Copyright 2004 by The Institute of Internal Auditors, Inc., 247 Maitland Avenue, Altamonte Springs, Florida 32710-4201 U.S.A. Reprinted with permission.

auditors are to be met. If internal auditors are prohibited by laws or regulations from complying with certain parts of the Standards, they should comply with all other parts of the Standards and make appropriate disclosures.

Assurance services involve the internal auditor's objective assessment of evidence to provide an independent opinion or conclusions regarding a process, system or other subject matter. The nature and scope of the assurance engagements are determined by the internal auditor. There are generally three parties involved in assurance services: 1) the person or group directly involved with the process, system or other subject matter—the process owner, 2) the person or group making the assessment—the internal auditor, and 3) the person or group using the assessment—the user.

Consulting services are advisory in nature and are generally performed at the specific request of an engagement client. The nature and scope of the consulting engagement are subject to agreement with the engagement client. Consulting services generally involve two parties: 1) the person or group offering the advice—the internal auditor, and 2) the person or group seeking and receiving the advice—the engagement client. When performing consulting services, the internal auditor should maintain objectivity and not assume management responsibility.

The Standards consist of Attribute Standards, Performance Standards, and Implementation Standards. The Attribute Standards address the characteristics of organizations and parties performing internal audit activities. The Performance Standards describe the nature of internal audit activities and provide quality criteria against which the performance of these services can be evaluated. While the Attribute and Performance Standards apply to all internal audit services, the Implementation Standards apply to specific types of engagements.

The Standards are part of the Professional Practices Framework. The Professional Practices Framework includes the Definition of Internal Auditing, the Code of Ethics, the Standards, and other guidance. Guidance regarding how the Standards might be applied is included in Practice Advisories that are issued by the Professional Issues Committee.

The development and issuance of Standards is an ongoing process. The Internal Auditing Standards Board engages in extensive consultation and discussion prior to issuance of the Standards. This includes worldwide solicitation for public comment through the exposure draft process.

ATTRIBUTE STANDARD 1200—PROFICIENCY AND DUE PROFESSIONAL CARE

Engagements should be performed with proficiency and due professional care.

1210—Proficiency

Internal auditors should possess the knowledge, skills, and other competencies needed to perform their individual responsibilities. The internal audit activity collectively should possess or obtain the knowledge, skills and other competencies needed to perform its responsibilities.

1210.A1—The chief audit executive should obtain competent advice and assistance if the internal audit staff lacks the knowledge, skills or other competencies needed to perform all or part of the engagement.

1210.A2—The internal auditor should have sufficient knowledge to identify the indicators of fraud but is not expected to have the expertise of a person whose primary responsibility is detecting and investigating fraud.

1210.A3—Internal auditors should have knowledge of key information technology risks and controls and available technology-based audit techniques to perform their assigned work. However, not all internal auditors are expected to have the expertise of an internal auditor whose primary responsibility is information technology auditing.

1210.C1—The chief audit executive should decline the consulting engagement or obtain competent advice and assistance if the internal audit staff lacks the knowledge, skills or other competencies needed to perform all or part of the engagement.

PERFORMANCE STANDARD 2100—
NATURE OF WORK

The internal audit activity should evaluate and contribute to the improvement of risk management, control, and governance processes using a systematic and disciplined approach.

2110—Risk Management

The internal audit activity should assist the organization by identifying and evaluating significant exposures to risk and contributing to the improvement of risk management and control systems.

2110.A1—The internal audit activity should monitor and evaluate the effectiveness of the organization's risk management system.

2110.A2—The internal audit activity should evaluate risk exposures relating to the organization's governance, operations, and information systems regarding the:

- Reliability and integrity of financial and operational information
- Effectiveness and efficiency of operations
- Safeguarding of assets
- Compliance with laws, regulations, and contracts

2110.C1—During consulting engagements, internal auditors should address risk consistent with the engagement's objectives and be alert to the existence of other significant risks.

2110.C2—Internal auditors should incorporate knowledge of risks gained from consulting engagements into the process of identifying and evaluating significant risk exposures of the organization.

PERFORMANCE STANDARD 2400—
COMMUNICATING RESULTS

Internal auditors should communicate the engagement results.

2410—Criteria for Communicating

Communications should include the engagement's objectives and scope as well as applicable conclusions, recommendations, and action plans.

2410.A1—Final communication of engagement results should, where appropriate, contain the internal auditor's overall opinion and/or conclusions.

2410.A2—Internal auditors are encouraged to acknowledge satisfactory performance in engagement communications.

2410.A3—When releasing engagement results to parties outside the organization, the communication should include limitations on distribution and use of results.

2410.C1—Communication of the progress and results of consulting engagements will vary in form and content depending upon the nature of the engagement and the needs of the client.

2420—Quality of Communications

Communications should be accurate, objective, clear, concise, constructive, complete, and timely.

2421—Errors and Omissions

If a final communication contains a significant error or omission, the chief audit executive should communicate corrected information to all parties who received the original communication.

2430—Engagement Disclosure of Noncompliance with the Standards

When noncompliance with the Standards impacts a specific engagement, communication of the results should disclose the:

- Standard (s) with which full compliance was not achieved
- Reason (s) for noncompliance
- Impact of noncompliance on the engagement

SARBANES-OXLEY ACT OF 2002

Section 204

Auditor Reports to Audit Committees

Section 10A of the Securities Exchange Act of 1934 (15 U.S.C. 78j-1), as amended by this Act, is amended by adding at the end the following:

(k) REPORTS TO AUDIT COMMITTEES—Each registered public accounting firm that performs for any issuer any audit required by this title shall timely report to the audit committee of the issuer—

(1) all critical accounting policies and practices to be used;

(2) all alternative treatments of financial information within generally accepted accounting principles that have been discussed with management officials of the issuer, ramifications of the use of such alternative disclosures and treatments, and the treatment preferred by the registered public accounting firm; and

(3) other material written communications between the registered public accounting firm and the management of the issuer, such as any management letter or schedule of unadjusted differences.

Section 302

Corporate Responsibility for Financial Reports

(a) REGULATIONS REQUIRED—The Commission shall, by rule, require, for each company filing periodic reports under section 13 (a) or 15 (d) of the Securities and Exchange Act of 1934 (15 U.S.C. 78m, 78o(d), that the principal executive officer or officers and the principal financial officer or officers, or persons performing similar functions, certify in each annual or quarterly report filed or submitted under either such section of such Act that

1) the signing officer has reviewed the report

2) based on the officer's knowledge, the report does not contain any untrue statement of a material fact or omit to state a

material fact necessary in order to make the statements made, in light of the circumstances under which such statements were made, not misleading

3) based on such officer's knowledge, the financial statements, and other financial information included in the report, fairly present in all material respects the financial condition and results of operations of the issuer as of, and for, the periods presented in the report

4) the signing officers

  A) are responsible for establishing and maintaining internal controls

  B) have designed such internal controls to ensure that material information relating to the issuer and its consolidated subsidiaries is made known to such officers by others within those entities, particularly during the period in which the periodic reports are being prepared

  C) have evaluated the effectiveness of the issuer's internal controls as of a date within 9 days prior to the report

  D) have presented in their report their conclusions about the effectiveness of their internal controls based on their evaluation as of that date

5) the signing officers have disclosed to the issuer's auditors and the audit committee of the board of directors (or persons fulfilling the equivalent function)

  A) all significant deficiencies in the design or operation of internal controls which could adversely affect the issuer's ability to record, process, summarize, and report financial data and have identified for the issuer's auditors any material weaknesses in internal controls

  B) any fraud, whether or not material, that involves management or other employees who have a significant role in the issuer's internal controls

6) the signing officers have indicated in the report whether or not there were significant changes in internal controls or in other factors that could significantly affect internal controls

subsequent to the date of their evaluation, including any corrective actions with regard to significant deficiencies and material weaknesses.

(b) FOREIGN REINCORPORATIONS HAVE NO EFFECT— Nothing in this section 302 shall be interpreted or applied in any way to allow any issuer to lessen the legal force of the statement required under this section 302, by an issuer having reincorporated or having engaged in any other transaction that resulted in the transfer of the corporate domicile or offices of the issuer from inside the United States to outside of the United States.

(c) DEADLINE—The rules required by subsection (a) shall be effective not later than 30 days after the date of enactment of this Act.

Section 404

Management Assessment of Internal Controls

(a) RULES REQUIRED—The Commission shall prescribe rules requiring each annual report required by section 13 of the Securities Exchange Act of 1934 (15 U.S.C. 78m) to contain an internal control report, which shall—

  1) state the responsibility of management for establishing and maintaining an adequate internal control structure and procedures for financial reporting; and

  2) contain an assessment, as of the end of the most recent fiscal year of the issuer, of the effectiveness of the internal control structure and procedures of the issuer for financial reporting.

(b) INTERNAL CONTROL EVALUATION AND REPORTING— With respect to the internal control assessment required by subsection (a), each registered public accounting firm that prepares or issues the audit report for the issuer shall attest to, and report on, the assessment made by the management of the issuer. An attestation made under this subsection shall be made in accordance with standards for attestation engagements issued or adopted by the Board. Any such attestation shall not be the subject of a separate engagement.

PUBLIC COMPANY ACCOUNTING OVERSIGHT BOARD

Selections from Bylaws and Rules—Standards—AS2

Auditor's Objective in an Audit of Internal Control Over Financial Reporting

4. The auditor's objective in an audit of internal control over financial reporting is to express an opinion on management's assessment of the effectiveness of the company's internal control over financial reporting. To form a basis for expressing such an opinion, the auditor must plan and perform the audit to obtain reasonable assurance about whether the company maintained, in all material respects, effective internal control over financial reporting as of the date specified in management's assessment.

   The auditor also must audit the company's financial statements as of the date specified in management's assessment because the information the auditor obtains during a financial statement audit is relevant to the auditor's conclusion about the effectiveness of the company's internal control over financial reporting. Maintaining effective internal control over financial reporting means that no material weaknesses exist; therefore, the objective of the audit of internal control over financial reporting is to obtain reasonable assurance that no material weaknesses exist as of the date specified in management's assessment.

5. To obtain reasonable assurance, the auditor evaluates the assessment performed by management and obtains and evaluates evidence about whether the internal control over financial reporting was designed and operated effectively. The auditor obtains this evidence from a number of sources, including using the work performed by others and performing auditing procedures himself or herself.

6. The auditor should be aware that persons who rely on the information concerning internal control over financial reporting

include investors, creditors, the board of directors and audit committee, and regulators in specialized industries, such as banking or insurance. The auditor should be aware that external users of financial statements are interested in information on internal control over financial reporting because it enhances the quality of financial reporting and increases their confidence in financial information, including financial information issued between annual reports, such as quarterly information. Information on internal control over financial reporting is also intended to provide an early warning to those inside and outside the company who are in a position to insist on improvements in internal control over financial reporting, such as the audit committee and regulators in specialized industries.

Additionally, Section 302 of the Act and Securities Exchange Act Rule 13a-14(a) or 15d-14(a)—see 17 C.F.R. 240.13a-14(a) or 17 C.F.R. 240.15d-14(a), whichever applies, require management, with the participation of the principal executive and financial officers, to make quarterly and annual certifications with respect to the company's internal control over financial reporting.

Definitions Related to Internal Control over Financial Reporting

7. For purposes of management's assessment and the audit of internal control over financial reporting in this standard, *internal control over financial reporting* is defined as follows:

A process designed by, or under the supervision of, the company's principal executive and principal financial officers, or persons performing similar functions, and effected by the company's board of directors, management, and other personnel, to provide reasonable assurance regarding the reliability of financial reporting and the preparation of financial statements for external purposes in accordance with generally accepted accounting principles and includes those policies and procedures that:

(1) Pertain to the maintenance of records that, in reasonable detail, accurately and fairly reflect the transactions and dispositions of the assets of the company;

(2) Provide reasonable assurance that transactions are recorded as necessary to permit preparation of financial statements in accordance with generally accepted accounting principles, and that receipts and expenditures of the company are being made only in accordance with authorizations of management and directors of the company; and

(3) Provide reasonable assurance regarding prevention or timely detection of unauthorized acquisition, use or disposition of the company's assets that could have a material effect on the financial statements.

Note: This definition is the same one used by the SEC in its rules requiring management to report on internal control over financial reporting, except the word "registrant" has been changed to "company" to conform to the wording in this standard. (see Securities Exchange Act Rules 13a-15(f) and 15d-15(f)—See 17 C.F.R. 240, 13a-15(f) and 15d-15(f).)

Note: Throughout this standard, *internal control over financial reporting* (singular) refers to the process described in this paragraph. Individual controls or subsets of controls are referred to as *controls* or *controls over financial reporting.*

8. A *control deficiency* exists when the design or operation of a control does not allow management or employees, in the normal course of performing their assigned functions, to prevent or detect misstatements on a timely basis.

   ○ A deficiency in *design* exists when (a) a control necessary to meet the control objective is missing or (b) an existing control is not properly designed so that, even if the control operates as designed, the control objective is not always met.

  ∘ A deficiency in *operation* exists when a properly designed control does not operate as designed, or when the person performing the control does not possess the necessary authority or qualifications to perform the control effectively.

9. A *significant deficiency* is a control deficiency, or combination of control deficiencies, that adversely affects the company's ability to initiate, authorize, record, process, or report external financial data reliably in accordance with generally accepted accounting principles such that there is more than a remote likelihood that a misstatement of the company's annual or interim financial statements that is more than inconsequential will not be prevented or detected.

Note: The term "remote likelihood" as used in the definitions of *significant deficiency* and *material weakness* (paragraph 10) has the same meaning as the term "remote" as used in Financial Accounting Standards Board Statement No. 5, *Accounting for Contingencies* ("FAS No. 5"). Paragraph 3 of FAS No. 5 states: When a loss contingency exists, the likelihood that the future event or events will confirm the loss or impairment of an asset or the incurrence of a liability can range from probable to remote. This Statement uses the terms *probable, reasonably possible*, and *remote* to identify three areas within that range, as follows: a. *Probable*. The future event or events are likely to occur. b. *Reasonably possible*. The chance of the future event or events occurring is more than remote but less than likely. c. *Remote*. The chance of the future events or events occurring is slight. Therefore, the likelihood of an event is "more than remote" when it is either reasonably possible or probable.

Note: A misstatement is *inconsequential* if a reasonable person would conclude, after considering the possibility of further undetected misstatements, that the misstatement, either individually or when aggregated with other misstatements, would clearly be immaterial to the financial statements. If a reasonable person could not reach such a conclusion regarding a particular misstatement, that misstatement is *more than inconsequential.*

10. A *material weakness* is a significant deficiency, or combination of significant deficiencies, that results in more than a remote likelihood that a material misstatement of the annual or interim financial statements will not be prevented or detected.

Note: In evaluating whether a control deficiency exists and whether control deficiencies, either individually or in combination with other control deficiencies, are significant deficiencies or material weaknesses, the auditor should consider the definitions in paragraphs 8, 9 and 10, and the directions in paragraphs 130 through 137. As explained in paragraph 23, the evaluation of the materiality of the control deficiency should include both quantitative and qualitative considerations. Qualitative factors that might be important in this evaluation include the nature of the financial statement accounts and assertions involved and the reasonably possible future consequences of the deficiency. Furthermore, in determining whether a control deficiency or combination of deficiencies is a significant deficiency or a material weakness, the auditor should evaluate the effect of compensating controls and whether such compensating controls are effective.

11. Controls over financial reporting may be *preventive controls* or *detective controls.*

   ○ Preventive controls have the objective of preventing errors or fraud from occurring in the first place that could result in a misstatement of the financial statements.

   ○ Detective controls have the objective of detecting errors or fraud that have already occurred that could result in a misstatement of the financial statements.

12. Even well-designed controls that are operating as designed might not prevent a misstatement from occurring. However, this possibility may be countered by overlapping preventive controls or partially countered by detective controls. Therefore, effective

internal control over financial reporting often includes a combination of preventive and detective controls to achieve a specific control objective. The auditor's procedures as part of either the audit of internal control over financial reporting or the audit of the financial statements are not part of a company's internal control over financial reporting.

Performing an Audit of Internal Control over Financial Reporting

27. In an audit of internal control over financial reporting, the auditor must obtain sufficient competent evidence about the design and operating effectiveness of controls over all relevant financial statement assertions related to all significant accounts and disclosures in the financial statements. The auditor must plan and perform the audit to obtain reasonable assurance that deficiencies that, individually or in the aggregate, would represent material weaknesses are identified. Thus, the audit is not designed to detect deficiencies in internal control over financial reporting that, individually or in the aggregate, are less severe than a material weakness.

Because of the potential significance of the information obtained during the audit of the financial statements to the auditor's conclusions about the effectiveness of internal control over financial reporting, the auditor cannot audit internal control over financial reporting without also auditing the financial statements.

Note: However, the auditor may audit the financial statements without also auditing internal control over financial reporting, for example, in the case of certain initial public offerings by a company. See the discussion beginning at paragraph 145 for more information about the importance of auditing both internal control over financial reporting as well as the financial statements when the auditor is engaged to audit internal control over financial reporting.

28. The auditor must adhere to the general standards (see paragraphs 30 through 36) and fieldwork and reporting standards (see paragraph 37) in performing an audit of a company's internal control over financial reporting.

    This involves the following:

    a. Planning the engagement;

    b. Evaluating management's assessment process;

    c. Obtaining an understanding of internal control over financial reporting;

    d. Testing and evaluating design effectiveness of internal control over financial reporting;

    e. Testing and evaluating operating effectiveness of internal control over financial reporting; and

    f. Forming an opinion on the effectiveness of internal control over financial reporting.

29. Even though some requirements of this standard are set forth in a manner that suggests a sequential process, auditing internal control over financial reporting involves a process of gathering, updating, and analyzing information. Accordingly, the auditor may perform some of the procedures and evaluations described in this section on "Performing an Audit of Internal Control Over Financial Reporting" concurrently.

Applying General, Fieldwork, and Reporting Standards

30. The general standards (see AU sec. 150, *Generally Accepted Auditing Standards*) are applicable to an audit of internal control over financial reporting. These standards require technical training and proficiency as an auditor, independence in fact and appearance, and the exercise of due professional care, including professional skepticism.

31. *Technical Training and Proficiency.* To perform an audit of internal control over financial reporting, the auditor should have

competence in the subject matter of internal control over financial reporting.

32. *Independence.* The applicable requirements of independence are largely predicated on four basic principles: (1) an auditor must not act as management or as an employee of the audit client, (2) an auditor must not audit his or her own work, (3) an auditor must not serve in a position of being an advocate for his or her client, and (4) an auditor must not have mutual or conflicting interests with his or her audit client. (See the Preliminary Note of Rule 2-01 of Regulation S-X, 17 C.F.R. 210.2-01.) If the auditor were to design or implement controls, that situation would place the auditor in a management role and result in the auditor auditing his or her own work. These requirements, however, do not preclude the auditor from making substantive recommendations as to how management may improve the design or operation of the company's internal controls as a by-product of an audit.

33. The auditor must not accept an engagement to provide internal control-related services to an issuer for which the auditor also audits the financial statements unless that engagement has been specifically pre-approved by the audit committee. For any internal control services the auditor provides, management must be actively involved and cannot delegate responsibility for these matters to the auditor. Management's involvement must be substantive and extensive. Management's acceptance of responsibility for documentation and testing performed by the auditor does not by itself satisfy the independence requirements.

34. Maintaining independence, in fact and appearance, requires careful attention, as is the case with all independence issues when work concerning internal control over financial reporting is performed. Unless the auditor and the audit committee are diligent in evaluating the nature and extent of services provided, the services might violate basic principles of independence and cause an impairment of independence in fact or appearance.

35. The independent auditor and the audit committee have significant and distinct responsibilities for evaluating whether the auditor's services impair independence in fact or appearance. The test for independence in fact is whether the activities would impede the ability of anyone on the engagement team or in a position to influence the engagement team from exercising objective judgment in the audits of the financial statements or internal control over financial reporting. The test for independence in appearance is whether a reasonable investor, knowing all relevant facts and circumstances, would perceive an auditor as having interests which could jeopardize the exercise of objective and impartial judgments on all issues encompassed within the auditor's engagement.

36. *Due Professional Care.* The auditor must exercise due professional care in an audit of internal control over financial reporting. One important tenet of due professional care is exercising professional skepticism. In an audit of internal control over financial reporting, exercising professional skepticism involves essentially the same considerations as in an audit of financial statements, that is, it includes a critical assessment of the work that management has performed in evaluating and testing controls.

37. *Fieldwork and Reporting Standards.* This standard establishes the fieldwork and reporting standards applicable to an audit of internal control over financial reporting.

38. The concept of materiality, as discussed in paragraphs 22 and 23, underlies the application of the general and fieldwork standards.

Planning the Engagement

39. The audit of internal control over financial reporting should be properly planned and assistants, if any, are to be properly supervised. When planning the audit of internal control over financial reporting, the auditor should evaluate how the following matters will affect the auditor's procedures:

- ○ Knowledge of the company's internal control over financial reporting obtained during other engagements.
- ○ Matters affecting the industry in which the company operates, such as financial reporting practices, economic conditions, laws and regulations, and technological changes.
- ○ Matters relating to the company's business, including its organization, operating characteristics, capital structure, and distribution methods.
- ○ The extent of recent changes, if any, in the company, its operations, or its internal control over financial reporting.
- ○ Management's process for assessing the effectiveness of the company's internal control over financial reporting based upon control criteria.
- ○ Preliminary judgments about materiality, risk, and other factors relating to the determination of material weaknesses.
- ○ Control deficiencies previously communicated to the audit committee or management.
- ○ Legal or regulatory matters of which the company is aware.
- ○ The type and extent of available evidence related to the effectiveness of the company's internal control over financial reporting.
- ○ Preliminary judgments about the effectiveness of internal control over financial reporting.
- ○ The number of significant business locations or units, including management's documentation and monitoring of controls over such locations or business units. (Appendix B, paragraphs B1 through B17, discusses factors the auditor should evaluate to determine the locations at which to perform auditing procedures.)

Obtaining an Understanding of Internal Control over Financial Reporting

47. The auditor should obtain an understanding of the design of specific controls by applying procedures that include:

- ○ Making inquiries of appropriate management, supervisory, and staff personnel;
- ○ Inspecting company documents;
- ○ Observing the application of specific controls; and
- ○ Tracing transactions through the information system relevant to financial reporting.

48. The auditor could also apply additional procedures to obtain an understanding of the design of specific controls.

49. The auditor must obtain an understanding of the design of controls related to each component of internal control over financial reporting, as discussed below.

- ○ *Control Environment.* Because of the pervasive effect of the control environment on the reliability of financial reporting, the auditor's preliminary judgment about its effectiveness often influences the nature, timing, and extent of the tests of operating effectiveness considered necessary. Weaknesses in the control environment should cause the auditor to alter the nature, timing, or extent of tests of operating effectiveness that otherwise should have been performed in the absence of the weaknesses.

- ○ *Risk Assessment.* When obtaining an understanding of the company's risk assessment process, the auditor should evaluate whether management has identified the risks of material misstatement in the significant accounts and disclosures and related assertions of the financial statements and has implemented controls to prevent or detect errors or fraud that could result in material misstatements. For example, the risk assessment process should address how management considers the possibility of unrecorded transactions or identifies and analyzes significant estimates recorded in the financial statements. Risks relevant to reliable financial reporting also relate to specific events or transactions.

- ○ *Control Activities.* The auditor's understanding of control activities relates to the controls that management has implemented to prevent or detect errors or fraud that could result in material misstatement in the accounts and disclosures and related assertions of the financial statements. For the purposes of evaluating the effectiveness of internal control over financial reporting, the auditor's understanding of control activities encompasses a broader range of accounts and disclosures than what is normally obtained for the financial statement audit.

- ○ *Information and Communication.* The auditor's understanding of management's information and communication involves understanding the same systems and processes that he or she addresses in an audit of financial statements. In addition, this understanding includes a greater emphasis on comprehending the safeguarding controls and the processes for authorization of transactions and the maintenance of records, as well as the period-end financial reporting process (discussed further beginning at paragraph 76).

- ○ *Monitoring.* The auditor's understanding of management's monitoring of controls extends to and includes its monitoring of all controls, including control activities, which management has identified and designed to prevent or detect material misstatement in the accounts and disclosures and related assertions of the financial statements.

50. Some controls (such as company-level controls, described in paragraph 53) might have a pervasive effect on the achievement of many overall objectives of the control criteria. For example, information technology general controls over program development, program changes, computer operations, and access to programs and data help ensure that specific controls over the processing of transactions are operating effectively. In contrast, other controls are designed to achieve specific objectives of the control criteria. For example, management generally establishes specific

controls, such as accounting for all shipping documents, to ensure that all valid sales are recorded.

51. The auditor should focus on combinations of controls, in addition to specific controls in isolation, in assessing whether the objectives of the control criteria have been achieved. The absence or inadequacy of a specific control designed to achieve the objectives of a specific criterion might not be a deficiency if other controls specifically address the same criterion. Further, when one or more controls achieve the objectives of a specific criterion, the auditor might not need to evaluate other controls designed to achieve those same objectives.

52. *Identifying Company-Level Controls.* Controls that exist at the company-level often have a pervasive impact on controls at the process, transaction, or application level. For that reason, as a practical consideration, it may be appropriate for the auditor to test and evaluate the design effectiveness of company-level controls first, because the results of that work might affect the way the auditor evaluates the other aspects of internal control over financial reporting.

53. Company-level controls are controls such as the following:

- Controls within the control environment, including tone at the top, the assignment of authority and responsibility, consistent policies and procedures, and company-wide programs, such as codes of conduct and fraud prevention, that apply to all locations and business units;
- Management's risk assessment process;
- Centralized processing and controls, including shared service environments;
- Controls to monitor results of operations;
- Controls to monitor other controls, including activities of the internal audit function, the audit committee, and self-assessment programs;
- The period-end financial reporting process; and

◦ Board-approved policies that address significant business control and risk management practices.

Note: The controls listed above are not intended to be a complete list of company-level controls nor is a company required to have all the controls in the list to support its assessment of effective company-level controls. However, ineffective company-level controls are a deficiency that will affect the scope of work performed, particularly when a company has multiple locations or business units, as described in Appendix B.

54. Testing company-level controls alone is not sufficient for the purpose of expressing an opinion on the effectiveness of a company's internal control over financial reporting.

55. Evaluating the Effectiveness of the Audit Committee's Oversight of the Company's External Financial Reporting and Internal Control Over Financial Reporting.

The company's audit committee plays an important role within the control environment and monitoring components of internal control over financial reporting. Within the control environment, the existence of an effective audit committee helps to set a positive tone at the top. Within the monitoring component, an effective audit committee challenges the company's activities in the financial arena.

Note: Although the audit committee plays an important role within the control environment and monitoring components of internal control over financial reporting, management is responsible for maintaining effective internal control over financial reporting. This standard does not suggest that this responsibility has been transferred to the audit committee.

Note: If no such committee exists with respect to the company, all references to the audit committee in this standard apply to the entire board of directors of the company. (See 15 U.S.C. 78c(a)58 and 15 U.S.C. 7201(a)(3).) The auditor should be aware that companies whose securities are not listed on a national securities exchange or an automated inter-dealer quotation system of a national securities association (such as the New York Stock Exchange, American Stock Exchange, or NASDAQ) may not be required to have independent directors for their audit committees. In this case, the auditor should not consider the lack of independent directors at these companies indicative, by itself, of a control deficiency. Likewise, the independence requirements of Securities Exchange Act Rule 10A-3 (see 17 C.F.R. 240.10A-3) are not applicable to the listing of non-equity securities of a consolidated or at least 50 percent beneficially owned subsidiary of a listed issuer that is subject to the requirements of Securities Exchange Act Rule 10A-3(c)(2)—see 17 C.F.R. 240.10A-3(c)(2). Therefore, the auditor should interpret references to the audit committee in this standard, as applied to a subsidiary registrant, as being consistent with the provisions of Securities Exchange Act Rule 10A-3(c)(2)—(see 17 C.F.R. 240.10A-3(c)(2). Furthermore, for subsidiary registrants, communications required by this standard to be directed to the audit committee should be made to the same committee or equivalent body that pre-approves the retention of the auditor by or on behalf of the subsidiary registrant pursuant to Rule 2-01(c)(7) of Regulation S-X—see 17 C.F.R. 210.2-01(c)(7)—(which might be, for example, the audit committee of the subsidiary registrant, the full board of the subsidiary registrant, or the audit committee of the subsidiary registrant's parent). In all cases, the auditor should interpret the terms "board of directors" and "audit committee" in this standard as being consistent with provisions for the use of those terms as defined in relevant SEC rules.

56. The company's board of directors is responsible for evaluating the performance and effectiveness of the audit committee; this standard does not suggest that the auditor is responsible for performing a separate and distinct evaluation of the audit committee. However, because of the role of the audit committee within the control environment and monitoring components of internal control over financial reporting, the auditor should assess the

effectiveness of the audit committee as part of understanding and evaluating those components.

57. The aspects of the audit committee's effectiveness that are important may vary considerably with the circumstances. The auditor focuses on factors related to the effectiveness of the audit committee's oversight of the company's external financial reporting and internal control over financial reporting, such as the independence of the audit committee members from management and the clarity with which the audit committee's responsibilities are articulated (for example, in the audit committee's charter) and how well the audit committee and management understand those responsibilities. The auditor might also consider the audit committee's involvement and interaction with the independent auditor and with internal auditors, as well as interaction with key members of financial management, including the chief financial officer and chief accounting officer.

58. The auditor might also evaluate whether the right questions are raised and pursued with management and the auditor, including questions that indicate an understanding of the critical accounting policies and judgmental accounting estimates, and the responsiveness to issues raised by the auditor.

59. Ineffective oversight by the audit committee of the company's external financial reporting and internal control over financial reporting should be regarded as at least a significant deficiency and is a strong indicator that a material weakness in internal control over financial reporting exists.

60. *Identifying Significant Accounts.* The auditor should identify significant accounts and disclosures, first at the financial-statement level and then at the account or disclosure-component level. Determining specific controls to test begins by identifying significant accounts and disclosures within the financial statements. When identifying significant accounts, the auditor should evaluate both quantitative and qualitative factors.

61. An account is significant if there is more than a remote likelihood that the account could contain misstatements that individually, or when aggregated with others, could have a material effect on the financial statements, considering the risks of both overstatement and understatement. Other accounts may be significant on a qualitative basis based on the expectations of a reasonable user. For example, investors might be interested in a particular financial statement account even though it is not quantitatively large because it represents an important performance measure.

    Note: For purposes of determining significant accounts, the assessment as to likelihood should be made without giving any consideration to the effectiveness of internal control over financial reporting.

62. Components of an account balance subject to differing risks (inherent and control) or different controls should be considered separately as potential significant accounts. For instance, inventory accounts often consist of raw materials (purchasing process), work in process (manufacturing process), finished goods (distribution process), and an allowance for obsolescence.

63. In some cases, separate components of an account might be a significant account because of the company's organizational structure. For example, for a company that has a number of separate business units, each with different management and accounting processes, the accounts at each separate business unit are considered individually as potential significant accounts.

64. An account also may be considered significant because of the exposure to unrecognized obligations represented by the account. For example, loss reserves related to a self-insurance program or unrecorded contractual obligations at a construction contracting subsidiary may have historically been insignificant in amount, yet might represent a more than remote likelihood of material misstatement due to the existence of material unrecorded claims.

65. When deciding whether an account is significant, it is important for the auditor to evaluate both quantitative and qualitative factors, including the:
    - Size and composition of the account;
    - Susceptibility of loss due to errors or fraud;
    - Volume of activity, complexity, and homogeneity of the individual transactions processed through the account;
    - Nature of the account (for example, suspense accounts generally warrant greater attention);
    - Accounting and reporting complexities associated with the account;
    - Exposure to losses represented by the account (for example, loss accruals related to a consolidated construction contracting subsidiary);
    - Likelihood (or possibility) of significant contingent liabilities arising from the activities represented by the account;
    - Existence of related party transactions in the account; and
    - Changes from the prior period in account characteristics (for example, new complexities or subjectivity or new types of transactions).

66. For example, in a financial statement audit, the auditor might not consider the fixed asset accounts significant when there is a low volume of transactions and when inherent risk is assessed as low, even though the balances are material to the financial statements. Accordingly, he or she might decide to perform only substantive procedures on such balances. In an audit of internal control over financial reporting, however, such accounts are significant accounts because of their materiality to the financial statements.

67. As another example, the auditor of the financial statements of a financial institution might not consider trust accounts significant to the institution's financial statements because such accounts are not included in the institution's balance sheet and the associated fee income generated by trust activities is not material. However, in determining whether trust accounts are a significant account

for purposes of the audit of internal control over financial reporting, the auditor should assess whether the activities of the trust department are significant to the institution's financial reporting, which also would include considering the contingent liabilities that could arise if a trust department failed to fulfill its fiduciary responsibilities (for example, if investments were made that were not in accordance with stated investment policies). When assessing the significance of possible contingent liabilities, consideration of the amount of assets under the trust department's control may be useful. For this reason, an auditor who has not considered trust accounts significant accounts for purposes of the financial statement audit might determine that they are significant for purposes of the audit of internal control over financial reporting.

68. Identifying Relevant Financial Statement Assertions. For each significant account, the auditor should determine the relevance of each of these financial statement assertions: (see AU sec. 326, *Evidential Matter*, which provides additional information on financial statement assertions.)

   - Existence or occurrence;
   - Completeness;
   - Valuation or allocation;
   - Rights and obligations; and
   - Presentation and disclosure.

69. To identify relevant assertions, the auditor should determine the source of likely potential misstatements in each significant account. In determining whether a particular assertion is relevant to a significant account balance or disclosure, the auditor should evaluate:

   - The nature of the assertion;
   - The volume of transactions or data related to the assertion; and
   - The nature and complexity of the systems, including the use of information technology by which the company processes and controls information supporting the assertion.

70. *Relevant assertions* are assertions that have a meaningful bearing on whether the account is fairly stated. For example, valuation may not be relevant to the cash account unless currency translation is involved; however, existence and completeness are always relevant. Similarly, valuation may not be relevant to the gross amount of the accounts receivable balance, but is relevant to the related allowance accounts. Additionally, the auditor might, in some circumstances, focus on the presentation and disclosure assertion separately in connection with the period-end financial reporting process.

71. *Identifying Significant Processes and Major Classes of Transactions.* The auditor should identify each significant process over each major class of transactions affecting significant accounts or groups of accounts. Major classes of transactions are those classes of transactions that are significant to the company's financial statements. For example, at a company whose sales may be initiated by customers through personal contact in a retail store or electronically through use of the internet, these types of sales would be two major classes of transactions within the sales process if they were both significant to the company's financial statements. As another example, at a company for which fixed assets is a significant account, recording depreciation expense would be a major class of transactions.

72. Different types of major classes of transactions have different levels of inherent risk associated with them and require different levels of management supervision and involvement.

   For this reason, the auditor might further categorize the identified major classes of transactions by transaction type: routine, non-routine, and estimation.

   ○ Routine transactions are recurring financial activities reflected in the accounting records in the normal course of business (for example, sales, purchases, cash receipts, cash disbursements, payroll).

   ○ Non-routine transactions are activities that occur only periodically (for example, taking physical inventory, calculating depreciation expense, adjusting for foreign currencies). A distinguishing feature of non-routine transactions is that data involved are generally not part of the routine flow of transactions.

- Estimation transactions are activities that involve management judgments or assumptions in formulating account balances in the absence of a precise means of measurement (for example, determining the allowance for doubtful accounts, establishing warranty reserves, assessing assets for impairment).

73. Most processes involve a series of tasks such as capturing input data, sorting and merging data, making calculations, updating transactions and master files, generating transactions, and summarizing and displaying or reporting data. The processing procedures relevant for the auditor to understand the flow of transactions generally are those activities required to initiate, authorize, record, process and report transactions. Such activities include, for example, initially recording sales orders, preparing shipping documents and invoices, and updating the accounts receivable master file. The relevant processing procedures also include procedures for correcting and reprocessing previously rejected transactions and for correcting erroneous transactions through adjusting journal entries.

74. For each significant process, the auditor should:

- Understand the flow of transactions, including how transactions are initiated, authorized, recorded, processed, and reported.
- Identify the points within the process at which a misstatement—including a misstatement due to fraud—related to each relevant financial statement assertion could arise.
- Identify the controls that management has implemented to address these potential misstatements.
- Identify the controls that management has implemented over the prevention or timely detection of unauthorized acquisition, use, or disposition of the company's assets.

Note: The auditor frequently obtains the understanding and identifies the controls described above as part of his or her performance of walkthroughs (as described beginning in paragraph 79).

75. The nature and characteristics of a company's use of information technology in its information system affect the company's internal control over financial reporting. AU sec. 319, *Consideration of Internal Control in a Financial Statement Audit*, paragraphs 16 through .20, .30 through .32, and .77 through .79, discuss the effect of information technology on internal control over financial reporting.

76. *Understanding the Period-end Financial Reporting Process.* The period-end financial reporting process includes the following:
    ○ The procedures used to enter transaction totals into the general ledger;
    ○ The procedures used to initiate, authorize, record, and process journal entries in the general ledger;
    ○ Other procedures used to record recurring and nonrecurring adjustments to the annual and quarterly financial statements, such as consolidating adjustments, report combinations, and classifications; and
    ○ Procedures for drafting annual and quarterly financial statements and related disclosures.

77. As part of understanding and evaluating the period-end financial reporting process, the auditor should evaluate:
    ○ The inputs, procedures performed, and outputs of the processes the company uses to produce its annual and quarterly financial statements;
    ○ The extent of information technology involvement in each period-end financial reporting process element;
    ○ Who participates from management;
    ○ The number of locations involved;
    ○ Types of adjusting entries (for example, standard, nonstandard, eliminating, and consolidating); and
    ○ The nature and extent of the oversight of the process by appropriate parties, including management, the board of directors, and the audit committee.

78. The period-end financial reporting process is always a significant process because of its importance to financial reporting and to the auditor's opinions on internal control over financial reporting and the financial statements. The auditor's understanding of the company's period-end financial reporting process and how it interrelates with the company's other significant processes assists the auditor in identifying and testing controls that are the most relevant to financial statement risks.

79. *Performing Walkthroughs.* The auditor should perform at least one walkthrough for each major class of transactions (as identified in paragraph 71). In a walkthrough, the auditor traces a transaction from origination through the company's information systems until it is reflected in the company's financial reports. Walkthroughs provide the auditor with evidence to:

- Confirm the auditor's understanding of the process flow of transactions;
- Confirm the auditor's understanding of the design of controls identified for all five components of internal control over financial reporting, including those related to the prevention or detection of fraud;
- Confirm that the auditor's understanding of the process is complete by determining whether all points in the process at which misstatements related to each relevant financial statement assertion that could occur have been identified;
- Evaluate the effectiveness of the design of controls; and
- Confirm whether controls have been placed in operation.

   Note: The auditor can often gain an understanding of the transaction flow, identify and understand controls, and conduct the walkthrough simultaneously.

80. The auditor's walkthroughs should encompass the entire process of initiating, authorizing, recording, processing, and reporting individual transactions and controls for each of the significant processes identified, including controls intended to address the

risk of fraud. During the walkthrough, at each point at which important processing procedures or controls occur, the auditor should question the company's personnel about their understanding of what is required by the company's prescribed procedures and controls and determine whether the processing procedures are performed as originally understood and on a timely basis. (Controls might not be performed regularly but still be timely.) During the walkthrough, the auditor should be alert for exceptions to the company's prescribed procedures and controls.

81. While performing a walkthrough, the auditor should evaluate the quality of the evidence obtained and perform walkthrough procedures that produce a level of evidence consistent with the objectives listed in paragraph 79. Rather than reviewing copies of documents and making inquiries of a single person at the company, the auditor should follow the process flow of actual transactions using the same documents and information technology that company personnel use and make inquiries of relevant personnel involved in significant aspects of the process or controls. To corroborate information at various points in the walkthrough, the auditor might ask personnel to describe their understanding of the previous and succeeding processing or control activities and to demonstrate what they do. In addition, inquiries should include follow-up questions that could help identify the abuse of controls or indicators of fraud.

   Examples of follow-up inquiries include asking personnel:

   ◦ What they do when they find an error or what they are looking for to determine if there is an error (rather than simply asking them if they perform listed procedures and controls); what kind of errors they have found; what happened as a result of finding the errors, and how the errors were resolved. If the person being interviewed has never found an error, the auditor should evaluate whether that situation is due to good preventive controls or whether the individual performing the control lacks the necessary skills.

- Whether they have ever been asked to override the process or controls, and if so, to describe the situation, why it occurred, and what happened.

82. During the period under audit, when there have been significant changes in the process flow of transactions, including the supporting computer applications, the auditor should evaluate the nature of the change(s) and the effect on related accounts to determine whether to walk through transactions that were processed both before and after the change.

    Note: Unless significant changes in the process flow of transactions, including the supporting computer applications, make it more efficient for the auditor to prepare new documentation of a walkthrough, the auditor may carry his or her documentation forward each year, after updating it for any changes that have taken place.

83. *Identifying Controls to Test.* The auditor should obtain evidence about the effectiveness of controls (either by performing tests of controls himself or herself, or by using the work of others) for all relevant assertions related to all significant accounts and disclosures in the financial statements.

    After identifying significant accounts, relevant assertions, and significant processes, the auditor should evaluate the following to identify the controls to be tested:

    - Points at which errors or fraud could occur;
    - The nature of the controls implemented by management;
    - The significance of each control in achieving the objectives of the control criteria and whether more than one control achieves a particular objective or whether more than one control is necessary to achieve a particular objective; and
    - The risk that the controls might not be operating effectively. Factors that affect whether the control might not be operating effectively include the following:
      - Whether there have been changes in the volume or nature of transactions that might adversely affect control design or operating effectiveness;

- ◦ Whether there have been changes in the design of controls;
- ◦ The degree to which the control relies on the effectiveness of other controls (for example, the control environment or information technology general controls);
- ◦ Whether there have been changes in key personnel who perform the control or monitor its performance;
- ◦ Whether the control relies on performance by an individual or is automated; and
- ◦ The complexity of the control.

84. The auditor should clearly link individual controls with the significant accounts and assertions to which they relate.

85. The auditor should evaluate whether to test preventive controls, detective controls, or a combination of both for individual relevant assertions related to individual significant accounts. For instance, when performing tests of preventive and detective controls, the auditor might conclude that a deficient preventive control could be compensated for by an effective detective control and, therefore, not result in a significant deficiency or material weakness. For example, a monthly reconciliation control procedure, which is a detective control, might detect an out-of-balance situation resulting from an unauthorized transaction being initiated due to an ineffective authorization procedure, which is a preventive control. When determining whether the detective control is effective, the auditor should evaluate whether the detective control is sufficient to achieve the control objective to which the preventive control relates.

Note: Because effective internal control over financial reporting often includes a combination of preventive and detective controls, the auditor ordinarily will test a combination of both.

Required Communications in an Audit of Internal Control over Financial Reporting

207. The auditor must communicate in writing to management and the audit committee all significant deficiencies and material

weaknesses identified during the audit. The written communication should be made prior to the issuance of the auditor's report on internal control over financial reporting. The auditor's communication should distinguish clearly between those matters considered to be significant deficiencies and those considered to be material weaknesses, as defined in paragraphs 9 and 10, respectively.

208. If a significant deficiency or material weakness exists because the oversight of the company's external financial reporting and internal control over financial reporting by the company's audit committee is ineffective, the auditor must communicate that specific significant deficiency or material weakness in writing to the board of directors.

209. In addition, the auditor should communicate to management, in writing, all deficiencies in internal control over financial reporting (that is, those deficiencies in internal control over financial reporting that are of a lesser magnitude than significant deficiencies) identified during the audit and inform the audit committee when such a communication has been made. When making this communication, it is not necessary for the auditor to repeat information about such deficiencies that have been included in previously issued written communications, whether those communications were made by the auditor, internal auditors, or others within the organization. Furthermore, the auditor is not required to perform procedures sufficient to identify all control deficiencies; rather, the auditor should communicate deficiencies in internal control over financial reporting of which he or she is aware.

Note: As part of his or her evaluation of the effectiveness of internal control over financial reporting, the auditor should determine whether control deficiencies identified by internal auditors and others within the company, for example, through ongoing monitoring activities and the annual assessment of internal control over financial reporting, are reported to appropriate levels of management in a timely manner. The lack of an internal process to report deficiencies in internal control to management on a timely basis represents a control deficiency that the auditor should evaluate as to severity.

210. These written communications should state that the communication is intended solely for the information and use of the board of directors, audit committee, management, and others within the organization. When there are requirements established by governmental authorities to furnish such reports, specific reference to such regulatory agencies may be made.

211. These written communications also should include the definitions of control deficiencies, significant deficiencies, and material weaknesses and should clearly distinguish to which category the deficiencies being communicated relate.

212. Because of the potential for misinterpretation of the limited degree of assurance associated with the auditor issuing a written report representing that no significant deficiencies were noted during an audit of internal control over financial reporting, the auditor should not issue such representations.

213. When auditing internal control over financial reporting, the auditor may become aware of fraud or possible illegal acts. If the matter involves fraud, it must be brought to the attention of the appropriate level of management. If the fraud involves senior management, the auditor must communicate the matter directly to the audit committee as described in AU sec. 316, *Consideration of Fraud in a Financial Statement Audit*. If the matter involves possible illegal acts, the auditor must assure himself or herself that the audit committee is adequately informed, unless the matter is clearly inconsequential, in accordance with AU sec. 317, *Illegal Acts by Clients*. The auditor also must determine his or her responsibilities under Section 10A of the Securities Exchange Act of 1934.

214. When timely communication is important, the auditor should communicate the preceding matters during the course of the audit rather than at the end of the engagement. The decision about

whether to issue an interim communication should be determined based on the relative significance of the matters noted and the urgency of corrective follow-up action required.

BYLAWS AND RULES—STANDARDS—AS3

As of February 10, 2006

Auditing and Related Professional Practice Standards

Auditing Standard No. 3, *Audit Documentation* [supersedes SAS No. 96, *Audit Documentation*]

INTRODUCTION

1. This standard establishes general requirements for documentation the auditor should prepare and retain in connection with engagements conducted pursuant to the standards of the Public Company Accounting Oversight Board ("PCAOB"). Such engagements include an audit of financial statements, an audit of internal control over financial reporting, and a review of interim financial information. This standard does not replace specific documentation requirements of other standards of the PCAOB.

OBJECTIVES OF AUDIT DOCUMENTATION

2. *Audit documentation* is the written record of the basis for the auditor's conclusions that provides the support for the auditor's representations, whether those representations are contained in the auditor's report or otherwise. Audit documentation also facilitates the planning, performance, and supervision of the engagement, and is the basis for the review of the quality of the work because it provides the reviewer with written documentation of the evidence supporting the auditor's significant conclusions. Among

other things, audit documentation includes records of the planning and performance of the work, the procedures performed, evidence obtained, and conclusions reached by the auditor. Audit documentation also may be referred to as *work papers* or *working papers*.

Note: An auditor's representations to a company's board of directors or audit committee, stockholders, investors, or other interested parties are usually included in the auditor's report accompanying the financial statements of the company. The auditor also might make oral representations to the company or others, either on a voluntary basis or if necessary to comply with professional standards, including in connection with an engagement for which an auditor's report is not issued. For example, although an auditor might not issue a report in connection with an engagement to review interim financial information, he or she ordinarily would make oral representations about the results of the review.

3. Audit documentation is reviewed by members of the engagement team performing the work and might be reviewed by others. Reviewers might include, for example:

   a. Auditors who are new to an engagement and review the prior year's documentation to understand the work performed as an aid in planning and performing the current engagement.

   b. Supervisory personnel who review documentation prepared by assistants on the engagement.

   c. Engagement supervisors and engagement quality reviewers who review documentation to understand how the engagement team reached significant conclusions and whether there is adequate evidential support for those conclusions.

   d. A successor auditor who reviews a predecessor auditor's audit documentation.

   e. Internal and external inspection teams that review documentation to assess audit quality and compliance with auditing and related professional practice standards; applicable laws, rules, and regulations; and the auditor's own quality control policies.

f. Others, including advisors engaged by the audit committee or representatives of a party to an acquisition.

AUDIT DOCUMENTATION REQUIREMENT

4. The auditor must prepare audit documentation in connection with each engagement conducted pursuant to the standards of the PCAOB. Audit documentation should be prepared in sufficient detail to provide a clear understanding of its purpose, source, and the conclusions reached. Also, the documentation should be appropriately organized to provide a clear link to the significant findings or issues. (See paragraph 12 of this standard for a description of significant findings or issues.) Examples of audit documentation include memoranda, confirmations, correspondence, schedules, audit programs, and letters of representation. Audit documentation may be in the form of paper, electronic files, or other media.

5. Because audit documentation is the written record that provides the support for the representations in the auditor's report, it should:

   a. Demonstrate that the engagement complied with the standards of the PCAOB,

   b. Support the basis for the auditor's conclusions concerning every relevant financial statement assertion, and

   c. Demonstrate that the underlying accounting records agreed or reconciled with the financial statements.

6. The auditor must document the procedures performed, evidence obtained, and conclusions reached with respect to relevant financial statement assertions. (*Relevant financial statement assertions* are described in paragraphs 68-70 of PCAOB Auditing Standard No. 2, *An Audit of Internal Control Over Financial Reporting Performed in Conjunction with an Audit of Financial Statements.*) Audit documentation must clearly demonstrate that the work was in fact performed. This documentation requirement

applies to the work of all those who participate in the engagement as well as to the work of specialists the auditor uses as evidential matter in evaluating relevant financial statement assertions. Audit documentation must contain sufficient information to enable an experienced auditor, having no previous connection with the engagement:

a. To understand the nature, timing, extent, and results of the procedures performed, evidence obtained, and conclusions reached, and

b. To determine who performed the work and the date such work was completed as well as the person who reviewed the work and the date of such review.

Note: An *experienced auditor* has a reasonable understanding of audit activities and has studied the company's industry as well as the accounting and auditing issues relevant to the industry.

7. In determining the nature and extent of the documentation for a financial statement assertion, the auditor should consider the following factors:

   ○ Nature of the auditing procedure;

   ○ Risk of material misstatement associated with the assertion;

   ○ Extent of judgment required in performing the work and evaluating the results, for example, accounting estimates require greater judgment and commensurately more extensive documentation;

   ○ Significance of the evidence obtained to the assertion being tested; and

   ○ Responsibility to document a conclusion not readily determinable from the documentation of the procedures performed or evidence obtained. Application of these factors determines whether the nature and extent of audit documentation is adequate.

8. In addition to the documentation necessary to support the auditor's final conclusions, audit documentation must include information the auditor has identified relating to significant findings or issues that is inconsistent with or contradicts the auditor's final conclusions.

The relevant records to be retained include, but are not limited to, procedures performed in response to the information, and records documenting consultations on, or resolutions of, differences in professional judgment among members of the engagement team or between the engagement team and others consulted.

9. If, after the documentation completion date (defined in paragraph 15), the auditor becomes aware, as a result of a lack of documentation or otherwise, that audit procedures may not have been performed, evidence may not have been obtained, or appropriate conclusions may not have been reached, the auditor must determine, and if so demonstrate, that sufficient procedures were performed, sufficient evidence was obtained, and appropriate conclusions were reached with respect to the relevant financial statement assertions. To accomplish this, the auditor must have persuasive other evidence. Oral explanation alone does not constitute persuasive other evidence, but it may be used to clarify other written evidence.

   ○ If the auditor determines and demonstrates that sufficient procedures were performed, sufficient evidence was obtained, and appropriate conclusions were reached, but that documentation thereof is not adequate, then the auditor should consider what additional documentation is needed. In preparing additional documentation, the auditor should refer to paragraph 16.

   ○ If the auditor cannot determine or demonstrate that sufficient procedures were performed, sufficient evidence was obtained, or appropriate conclusions were reached, the auditor should comply with the provisions of AU sec. 390, *Consideration of Omitted Procedures After the Report Date*.

DOCUMENTATION OF SPECIFIC MATTERS

10. Documentation of auditing procedures that involve the inspection of documents or confirmation, including tests of details, tests of operating effectiveness of controls, and walkthroughs, should

include identification of the items inspected. Documentation of auditing procedures related to the inspection of significant contracts or agreements should include abstracts or copies of the documents.

Note: The identification of the items inspected may be satisfied by indicating the source from which the items were selected and the specific selection criteria, for example:

- If an audit sample is selected from a population of documents, the documentation should include identifying characteristics (for example, the specific check numbers of the items included in the sample).

- If all items over a specific dollar amount are selected from a population of documents, the documentation need describe only the scope and the identification of the population (for example, all checks over $10,000 from the October disbursements journal).

- If a systematic sample is selected from a population of documents, the documentation need only provide an identification of the source of the documents and an indication of the starting point and the sampling interval (for example, a systematic sample of sales invoices was selected from the sales journal for the period from October 1 to December 31, starting with invoice number 452 and selecting every 40th invoice).

11. Certain matters, such as auditor independence, staff training and proficiency and client acceptance and retention, may be documented in a central repository for the public accounting firm ("firm") or in the particular office participating in the engagement. If such matters are documented in a central repository, the audit documentation of the engagement should include a reference to the central repository. Documentation of matters specific to a particular engagement should be included in the audit documentation of the pertinent engagement.

12. The auditor must document significant findings or issues, actions taken to address them (including additional evidence obtained), and the basis for the conclusions reached in connection with each engagement. *Significant findings or issues* are substantive matters that are important to the procedures performed, evidence obtained, or conclusions reached, and include, but are not limited to, the following:

a. Significant matters involving the selection, application, and consistency of accounting principles, including related disclosures. Significant matters include, but are not limited to, accounting for complex or unusual transactions, accounting estimates, and uncertainties as well as related management assumptions.

b. Results of auditing procedures that indicate a need for significant modification of planned auditing procedures, the existence of material misstatements, omissions in the financial statements, the existence of significant deficiencies, or material weaknesses in internal control over financial reporting.

c. Audit adjustments. For purposes of this standard, an *audit adjustment* is a correction of a misstatement of the financial statements that was or should have been proposed by the auditor, whether or not recorded by management, that could, either individually or when aggregated with other misstatements, have a material effect on the company's financial statements.

d. Disagreements among members of the engagement team or with others consulted on the engagement about final conclusions reached on significant accounting or auditing matters.

e. Circumstances that cause significant difficulty in applying auditing procedures.

f. Significant changes in the assessed level of audit risk for particular audit areas and the auditor's response to those changes.

g. Any matters that could result in modification of the auditor's report.

13. The auditor must identify all significant findings or issues in an *engagement completion document*. This document may include either all information necessary to understand the significant findings, issues or cross-references, as appropriate, to other available supporting audit documentation. This document, along with any documents cross-referenced, should collectively be as specific as necessary in the circumstances for a reviewer to gain a thorough understanding of the significant findings or issues.

Note: The engagement completion document prepared in connection with the annual audit should include documentation of significant findings or issues identified during the review of interim financial information.

THE COMMITTEE OF SPONSORING ORGANIZATIONS OF THE TREADWAY COMMISSION (COSO)

http://www.coso.org/publications/executive_summary_integrated_framework.htm

INTERNAL CONTROL—INTEGRATED FRAMEWORK

Executive Summary

Senior executives have long sought ways to better control the enterprises they run. Internal controls are put in place to keep the company on course toward profitability goals and achievement of its mission, and to minimize surprises along the way. They enable management to deal with rapidly changing economic and competitive environments, shifting customer demands and priorities, and restructuring for future growth. Internal controls promote efficiency, reduce risk of asset loss, and help ensure the reliability of financial statements and compliance with laws and regulations.

Because internal control serves many important purposes, there are increasing calls for better internal control systems and report cards on them. Internal control is looked upon more and more as a solution to a variety of potential problems.

What Internal Control Is

Internal control means different things to different people. This causes confusion among businesspeople, legislators, regulators and others. Resulting miscommunication and different expectations cause problems within an enterprise. Problems are compounded when the term, if not clearly defined, is written into law, regulation or rule.

This report deals with the needs and expectations of management and others. It defines and describes internal control to:

- Establish a common definition serving the needs of different parties.
- Provide a standard against which business and other entities—large or small, in the public or private sector, for profit or not—can assess their control systems and determine how to improve them.

Internal control is broadly defined as a process, effected by an entity's board of directors, management and other personnel, designed to provide reasonable assurance regarding the achievement of objectives in the following categories:

- Effectiveness and efficiency of operations
- Reliability of financial reporting
- Compliance with applicable laws and regulations

The first category addresses an entity's basic business objectives, including performance and profitability goals and safeguarding of resources. The second relates to the preparation of reliable published financial statements, including interim and condensed financial statements and selected financial data derived from such statements, such as earnings releases, reported publicly. The third deals with complying with those laws and regulations to which the entity is subject. These distinct but overlapping categories address different needs and allow a directed focus to meet the separate needs.

Internal control systems operate at different levels of effectiveness. Internal control can be judged effective in each of the three categories, respectively, if the board of directors and management have reasonable assurance that:

- They understand the extent to which the entity's operations objectives are being achieved.
- Published financial statements are being prepared reliably.
- Applicable laws and regulations are being complied with.

While internal control is a process, its effectiveness is a state or condition of the process at one or more points in time.

Internal control consists of five interrelated components. These are derived from the way management runs a business, and are integrated with the management process. Although the components apply to all entities, small and mid-size companies may implement them differently than large ones. Its controls may be less formal and less structured, yet a small company can still have effective internal control. The components are:

Control Environment. The control environment sets the tone of an organization, influencing the control consciousness of its people. It is the foundation for all other components of internal control, providing discipline and structure. Control environment factors include the integrity, ethical values and competence of the entity's people; management's philosophy and operating style; the way management assigns authority and responsibility, and organizes and develops its people; and the attention and direction provided by the board of directors.

Risk Assessment. Every entity faces a variety of risks from external and internal sources that must be assessed. A precondition to risk assessment is establishment of objectives, linked at different levels and internally consistent. Risk assessment is the identification and analysis of relevant risks to achievement of the objectives, forming a basis for determining how the risks should be managed. Because economic, industry, regulatory and operating conditions will continue to change, mechanisms are needed to identify and deal with the special risks associated with change.

Control Activities. Control activities are the policies and procedures that help ensure management directives are carried out. They help ensure that necessary actions are taken to address risks to achievement of the entity's objectives. Control activities occur throughout the organization, at all levels and in all functions. They include a range of activities as diverse as approvals, authorizations, verifications, reconciliations, reviews of operating performance, security of assets and segregation of duties.

Information and Communication. Pertinent information must be identified, captured and communicated in a form and timeframe that enable people to carry out their responsibilities. Information systems produce reports, containing operational, financial and compliance-related information, that make it possible to run and control the business. They deal not only with internally generated data, but also information about external events, activities and conditions necessary to informed business decision-making and external reporting. Effective communication also must occur in a broader sense, flowing down, across and up the organization. All personnel must receive a clear message from top management that control responsibilities must be taken seriously. They must understand their own role in the internal control system, as well as how individual activities relate to the work of others. They must have a means of communicating significant information upstream. There also needs to be effective communication with external parties, such as customers, suppliers, regulators and shareholders.

Monitoring. Internal control systems need to be monitored—a process that assesses the quality of the system's performance over time. This is accomplished through ongoing monitoring activities, separate evaluations or a combination of the two. Ongoing monitoring occurs in the course of operations. It includes regular management and supervisory activities, and other actions personnel take in performing their duties. The scope and frequency of separate evaluations will depend primarily on an assessment of risks and the effectiveness of ongoing monitoring procedures. Internal control deficiencies should be reported upstream, with serious matters reported to top management and the board.

There is synergy and linkage among these components, forming an integrated system that reacts dynamically to changing conditions. The internal control system is intertwined with the entity's operating activities and exists for fundamental business reasons. Internal control is most effective when controls are built into the entity's infrastructure and are a part of the essence of the enterprise. "Built in" controls support quality and empowerment initiatives, avoid unnecessary costs and enable quick response to changing conditions.

There is a direct relationship between the three categories of objectives, which are what an entity strives to achieve, and components, which represent what is needed to achieve the objectives. All components are relevant to each objectives category. When looking at any one category—the effectiveness and efficiency of operations, for instance— all five components must be present and functioning effectively to conclude that internal control over operations is effective.

The internal control definition—with its underlying fundamental concepts of a process, effected by people, providing reasonable assurance—together with the categorization of objectives and the components and criteria for effectiveness, and the associated discussions, constitute this internal control framework.

What Internal Control Can Do

Internal control can help an entity achieve its performance and profitability targets, and prevent loss of resources. It can help ensure reliable financial reporting. And it can help ensure that the enterprise complies with laws and regulations, avoiding damage to its reputation and other consequences. In sum, it can help an entity get to where it wants to go, and avoid pitfalls and surprises along the way.

What Internal Control Cannot Do

Unfortunately, some people have greater, and unrealistic, expectations. They look for absolutes, believing that:

- Internal control can ensure an entity's success—that is, it will ensure achievement of basic business objectives or will, at the least, ensure survival.

  Even effective internal control can only help an entity achieve these objectives. It can provide management information about the entity's progress, or lack of it, toward their achievement. But internal control cannot change an inherently poor manager into a good one. And, shifts in government policy or programs, competitors' actions or economic conditions can be beyond management's control. Internal control cannot ensure success, or even survival.

- Internal control can ensure the reliability of financial reporting and compliance with laws and regulations.

  This belief is also unwarranted. An internal control system, no matter how well conceived and operated, can provide only reasonable—not absolute—assurance to management and the board regarding achievement of an entity's objectives. The likelihood of achievement is affected by limitations inherent in all internal control systems. These include the realities that judgments in decision-making can be faulty, and that breakdowns can occur because of simple error or mistake. Additionally, controls can be circumvented by the collusion of two or more people, and management has the ability to override the system. Another limiting factor is that the design of an internal control system must reflect the fact that there are resource constraints, and the benefits of controls must be considered relative to their costs.

Thus, while internal control can help an entity achieve its objectives, it is not a panacea.

Roles and Responsibilities

Everyone in an organization has responsibility for internal control.

Management

The chief executive officer is ultimately responsible and should assume "ownership" of the system. More than any other individual, the chief executive sets the "tone at the top" that affects integrity and ethics and other factors of a positive control environment. In a large company, the chief executive fulfills this duty by providing leadership and direction to senior managers and reviewing the way they're controlling the business. Senior managers, in turn, assign responsibility for establishment of more specific internal control policies and procedures to personnel responsible for the unit's functions. In a smaller entity, the influence of the chief executive, often an owner-manager, is usually more direct. In any event, in a cascading responsibility, a manager is effectively a chief executive of his or her sphere of responsibility. Of particular significance are financial officers and their staffs, whose control activities cut across, as well as up and down, the operating and other units of an enterprise.

Board of Directors

Management is accountable to the board of directors, which provides governance, guidance and oversight. Effective board members are objective, capable and inquisitive. They also have a knowledge of the entity's activities and environment, and commit the time necessary to fulfill their board responsibilities. Management may be in a position to override controls and ignore or stifle communications from subordinates, enabling a dishonest management, which intentionally misrepresents results to cover its tracks. A strong, active board, particularly when coupled with effective upward communications channels and capable financial, legal and internal audit functions, is often best able to identify and correct such a problem.

Internal Auditors

Internal auditors play an important role in evaluating the effectiveness of control systems, and contribute to ongoing effectiveness. Because of organizational position and authority in an entity, an internal audit function often plays a significant monitoring role.

Other Personnel

Internal control is, to some degree, the responsibility of everyone in an organization and therefore should be an explicit or implicit part of everyone's job description. Virtually all employees produce information used in the internal control system or take other actions needed to effect control. Also, all personnel should be responsible for communicating upward problems in operations, noncompliance with the code of conduct, or other policy violations or illegal actions.

A number of external parties often contribute to achievement of an entity's objectives. External auditors, bringing an independent and objective view, contribute directly through the financial statement audit and indirectly by providing information useful to management and the board in carrying out their responsibilities. Others providing information to the entity useful in effecting internal control are legislators and regulators, customers and others transacting business with the enterprise, financial analysts, bond raters and the news media. External parties, however, are not responsible for, nor are they a part of, the entity's internal control system.

Organization of this Report

This report is in four volumes. The first is this Executive Summary, a high-level overview of the internal control framework directed to the chief executive and other senior executives, board members, legislators and regulators.

The second volume, the Framework, defines internal control, describes its components and provides criteria against which managements, boards or others can assess their control systems. The Executive Summary is included.

The third volume, Reporting to External Parties, is a supplemental document providing guidance to those entities that report publicly on internal control over preparation of their published financial statements, or are contemplating doing so.

The fourth volume, Evaluation Tools, provides materials that may be useful in conducting an evaluation of an internal control system.

What to Do

Actions that might be taken as a result of this report depend on the position and role of the parties involved:

Senior Management

Most senior executives who contributed to this study believe they are basically "in control" of their organizations. Many said, however, that there are areas of their company—a division, a department or a control component that cuts across activities—where controls are in early stages of development or otherwise need to be strengthened. They do not like surprises. This study suggests that the chief executive initiate a self-assessment of the control system. Using this framework, a CEO, together with key operating and financial executives, can focus attention where needed. Under one approach, the chief executive could proceed by bringing together business unit heads and key functional staff to discuss an initial assessment of control. Directives would be provided for those individuals to discuss this report's concepts with their lead personnel, provide oversight of the initial assessment process in their areas of responsibility and report back findings. Another approach might involve an initial review of corporate and business unit policies and internal audit programs. Whatever its form, an initial self-assessment should determine whether there is a need for, and how to proceed with, a broader, more in-depth evaluation. It should also ensure that ongoing monitoring processes are in place. Time spent in evaluating internal control represents an investment, but one with a high return.

Board Members

Members of the board of directors should discuss with senior management the state of the entity's internal control system and provide oversight as needed. They should seek input from the internal and external auditors.

Other Personnel

Managers and other personnel should consider how their control responsibilities are being conducted in light of this framework, and discuss with more senior personnel ideas for strengthening control. Internal auditors should consider the breadth of their focus on the internal control system, and may wish to compare their evaluation materials to the evaluation tools.

Legislators and Regulators

Government officials who write or enforce laws recognize that there can be misconceptions and different expectations about virtually any issue. Expectations for internal control vary widely in two respects. First, they differ regarding what control systems can accomplish. As noted, some observers believe internal control systems will, or should, prevent economic loss, or at least prevent companies from going out of business. Second, even when there is agreement about what internal control systems can and can't do, and about the validity of the "reasonable assurance" concept, there can be disparate views of what that concept means and how it will be applied. Corporate executives have expressed concern regarding how regulators might construe public reports asserting "reasonable assurance" in hindsight after an alleged control failure has occurred. Before legislation or regulation dealing with management reporting on internal control is acted upon, there should be agreement on a common internal control framework, including limitations of internal control. This framework should be helpful in reaching such agreement.

Professional Organizations

Rule-making and other professional organizations providing guidance on financial management, auditing and related topics should consider their standards and guidance in light of this framework. To the extent diversity in concept and terminology is eliminated, all parties will benefit.

Educators

This framework should be the subject of academic research and analysis, to see where future enhancements can be made. With the presumption that this report becomes accepted as a common ground for understanding, its concepts and terms should find their way into university curricula.

We believe this report offers a number of benefits. With this foundation for mutual understanding, all parties will be able to speak a common language and communicate more effectively. Business executives will be positioned to assess control systems against a standard, and strengthen the systems and move their enterprises toward established goals. Future research can be leveraged off an established base. Legislators and regulators will be able to gain an increased understanding of internal control, its benefits and limitations. With all parties utilizing a common internal control framework, these benefits will be realized.

FIND THE FLAWS

VERB FLAWS

The verbs are misused in some way in the following 10 sentences, and other grammatical errors may also exist. Observe keenly, find the flaws, and fix them. Corrections follow!

1. Methods of improving site security had been developed by management which included documenting site security processes and to enforce security practices.
2. In three instances, responsibilities were not defined or included in the job description and were not signed by management.
3. Internal Audit assessed the security controls inherent in the software as part of this review and procedural internal controls were proposed.
4. If possible both the Vendor Master File and the payment file should be imported from the accounting system protecting the imported files from changes.
5. Internal Audit made an examination of how claims were processed focusing on effectiveness of existing procedures and adequacy of provisions.
6. Original invoices and receipts are the only acceptable forms of support for expense report items; credit card vouchers and photocopies risks duplicate payments.

7. The Receivables Accountant did not recognize three sets of job tickets during the month for which the job was being performed and approved due to the job tickets not being sent and reviewed by management on a timely basis.

8. May and June invoices had been counted and found that an average of 60% of the service reports contained wrong pricing information.

9. A process to track software licenses will be researched, developed, documented and implemented by IT management and performance of a full software inventory.

10. In conducting a review of procurement and inventory management, minor issues were detected but it was determined that these issues would not effect the company's ability to achieve its objectives.

Corrected versions:

1. Management developed two methods of improving site security: documentation of site security processes and enforcement of security practices.

2. In three instances, job descriptions were not signed by management and did not include definitions of responsibilities.

3. As part of this review, Internal Audit assessed the security controls inherent in the software and proposed procedural internal controls.

4. If possible, both the Vendor Master File and the payment file should be imported from the accounting system, and the imported files should be protected from changes.

5. Internal Audit examined how claims were processed and focused on effectiveness of existing procedures and adequacy of provisions.

6. Original invoices and receipts are the only acceptable forms of support for expense report items; credit card vouchers and photocopies run the risk of duplicate payments.

7. The Receivables Accountant did not recognize three sets of job tickets during the month for which the job was performed and approved because management did not review and send the job tickets on time.

8. A count of May and June invoices revealed that an average of 60% of the service reports contained inaccurate pricing information.

9. IT management will perform a full software inventory and will develop, document, and implement a process to track software licenses.

10. In our review of procurement and inventory management, we detected minor issues but determined that these issues would not affect the company's ability to achieve its objectives.

MODIFIER FLAWS

The following 10 sentences contain misplaced or expanded modifiers and could use some general editing. Observe, find, and fix the flaws! Corrections follow.

1. Certain privileged users in the Worldwide Finance Center can only access these control accounts.

2. Deferred revenue of USD 120,000 was recorded in the subsidiary books in Q3 2006, which could not be substantiated.

3. These prices are lump-sum and aggregate several services; however, the company position has been not to pay the total amounts, discounting amounts at time of payment related to services not rendered.

4. Due to recent systems enhancements, there were well-defined processes in procurement, accounts payable, and inventory management and complete and effective documentation in them but not in IT, site security and treasury.

5. It is important for the remote job entry site to have adequate controls in order to protect the entire network as an access point within the overall network.

6. Requests for the supporting documents were made to the branches and sent directly to Internal Audit upon request in Chicago.

7. The last depreciation provided was in December 2005 by a straight journal voucher for the following segments:

8. An employee independent of the system administration function should review the user IDs on a monthly basis to ensure all user IDs are current and have standard user profiles matrices unless otherwise authorized.

9. Internal Audit recommends that before each payment a report from MFG-Pro detailing all changes in the Vendor Master file since the last payment date should be reviewed and the changes verified to supporting documentation.

10. In its recent review, Internal Audit noted that the data storage facility that is located at Headquarters has security violations.

Corrected versions:

1. Only certain privileged users in the Worldwide Finance Center can access these control accounts.

2. Deferred revenue of USD 120,000, which could not be substantiated, was recorded in the subsidiary books in Q3 2006.

3. These prices are lump-sum and aggregate several services; however, the company position has been not to pay the total amounts, discounting amounts related to services not rendered at time of payment.

4. Due to recent systems enhancements, there were well-defined processes in procurement, accounts payable, and inventory management and complete and effective documentation in them but not in IT, site security, and treasury.

5. As an important network access point, the remote job entry site must have adequate controls in order to protect the entire network.

6. Requests for the supporting documents were made to the branches and sent directly to Internal Audit upon request in Chicago.

7. The last depreciation provided was in December 2005 by a straight journal voucher for the following segments:

8. An employee independent of the system administration function should review the user IDs on a monthly basis to ensure all user IDs are current and have standard user profiles matrices unless otherwise authorized.

9. Internal Audit recommends that before each payment a report from MFG-Pro detailing all changes in the Vendor Master file since the last payment date should be reviewed and the changes verified to supporting documentation.

10. Internal Audit noted security violations at the Headquarters data storage facility.

PUNCTUATION FLAWS

Tiny commas make big differences. Check out the following 10 sentences and fix the punctuation flaws and any other problems you observe. Corrections are below.

1. Where possible PCs should be kept in physically secure locations accessible only to authorized personnel.

2. Internal Audit reviewed and tested samples of Petty Cash, Revenue and Accounts Receivable, Employee Expense Reports, Fixed Assets and Maintenance and Spares.

3. Before a payment run is made any changes to the Vendor File should be reviewed.

4. Process definitions and documentation support control of the processes, and ensure that the organizations success is not dependent only on the skills of current personnel.

5. At the time of the review there was no link between the authentication diskette and the user ID of a Signatory.

6. This balance of USD 130,000 was outstanding since prior to 2005 and as per the location it was not expected to be recovered.

7. Reports including exceptions and timelines recommendations were not used to shift time and resources as recommended, and did not add time to the testing phase.

8. The balance sheet notes did not provide any details about the duration of the contracts and the location did not have this information or the reason for these bonds not to be amortized.

9. COSOs report outlines five key components of internal control 1) control environment 2) risk assessment 3) control activities 4) information and communication 5) and monitoring.

10. Section 404 also requires the company's auditor to attest to, and report on managements assessment of the effectiveness of the company's internal controls and procedures for financial reporting in accordance with standards established by the Public Company Accounting Oversight Board.

Corrected versions:

1. Where possible, PCs should be kept in physically secure locations accessible only to authorized personnel.

2. Internal Audit reviewed and tested samples of Petty Cash, Revenue and Accounts Receivable, Employee Expense Reports, Fixed Assets, and Maintenance and Spares.

3. Before a payment run is made, any changes to the Vendor File should be reviewed.

4. Process definitions and documentation support control of the processes and ensure that the organization's success is not dependent only on the skills of current personnel.

5. At the time of the review, there was no link between the authentication diskette and the user ID of a Signatory.

6. This balance of USD 130,000 was outstanding since before 2005 and, as stated by the location manager, it was not expected to be recovered.

7. Reports, including exceptions and timelines recommendations, were not used to shift time and resources, as recommended, and did not lengthen the testing phase.

8. The balance sheet notes did not provide any details about the duration of the contracts, and the location did not have this information—or the reason for these bonds not to be amortized.

9. COSO's report outlines five key components of internal control: (1) control environment, (2) risk assessment, (3) control activities, (4) information and communication, and (5) monitoring.

10. Section 404 also requires the company's auditor to attest to, and report on, management's assessment of the effectiveness of the company's internal controls and procedures for financial reporting, in accordance with standards established by the Public Company Accounting Oversight Board.

BIBLIOGRAPHY

Agnes, Michael, ed. *Webster's New World College Dictionary*, 4th
ed. New York: Macmillan, 1999.

Atkinson, Cliff. *Beyond Bullet Points*. Redmond, WA: Microsoft
Press, 2005.

Blake, Gary, and Robert W. Bly. *The Elements of Business Writing*.
New York: Collier Books, Macmillan, 1991.

Brown, John Seeley, and Paul Duguid. *The Social Life of
Information*. Boston: Harvard Business School Press, 2002.

Brusaw, Charles T., and Gerald J. Alred. *The Business Writer's
Handbook*. 5th ed. New York: St. Martin's Press, 1997.

Chapman, Robert L. *American Slang*, 2nd ed. New York:
HarperCollins, 1998.

Cutler, Sally F. *Designing and Writing Message-Based Audit Reports*.
Altamonte Springs, FL: The Institute of Internal Auditors, 2001.

Few, Stephen. *Show Me the Numbers*. Oakland, CA: Analytics Press,
2004.

Fowler, H.W. *A Dictionary of Modern English Usage*, 6th ed. New
York and Oxford: Oxford University Press, 1991.

Friedman, Thomas L. *The World Is Flat*. New York: Farrar, Straus,
and Giroux, 2005.

Goldstein, Norm, ed. *The Associated Press Stylebook and Libel
Manual*. New York: Addison-Wesley, 1996.

James, David L. *The Executive Guide to Asia-Pacific
Communications*. New York: Kodansha America, 1995.

Lefton, Robert E., Ph.D., and Victor R. Buzzotta, Ph.D. *Leadership through People Skills*. New York: McGraw-Hill, 2004.

Maniak, Angela J. *Report Writing for Internal Auditors*. New York: McGraw-Hill, 1990.

Pickett, K.H. Spencer. *Audit Planning: A Risk-Based Approach*. Hoboken, NJ: John Wiley & Sons, 2006.

Ramos, Michael. *How to Comply with Sarbanes-Oxley Section 404*. Hoboken, NJ: John Wiley & Sons, 2004.

Ranadive, Vivck. *The Power of Now*. New York: McGraw-Hill, 1999.

Shertzer, Margaret. *The Elements of Grammar*. New York: Macmillan, 1986.

Siegal, Allan M., and William G. Connolly. *The New York Times Manual of Style and Usage*. New York: Time Books, 1999.

Tarshis, Barry. *How to Be Your Own Best Editor*. New York: Three Rivers Press, 1998.

Tufte, Edward R. *The Visual Display of Quantitative Information*, 17th ed. Cheshire, CT: Graphics Press, 1999.

Wensberg, Eric. *Modern American Usage*. New York: Hill and Wang, 1998.

Wurman, Richard Saul. *Information Anxiety*. New York: Doubleday, 1989.

Zinsser, William. *On Writing Well*. New York: Harper & Row, 1985.

Zweifel, Thomas D., Ph.D., *Communicate or Die: Getting Results through Speaking and Listening*. New York: SelectBooks, 2003.

_____, *Culture Clash: Managing the Global High Performance Team*. New York: SelectBooks Inc., New York, NY, 2003.

INDEX

Access to information, 48
Accounting, 47, 48
Accuracy
  and automation, 44, 45, 47
  and editing process, 144
  executive certification, 91
  writing standards, 28, 29
Acronyms, use of, 58, 105, 106
Adjectives, 158. See also
      Modifiers
"Agree," use of with prepositions,
      125
AICPA. See American Institute of
      Certified Public Accountants
      (AICPA)
American Institute of Certified
      Public Accountants (AICPA)
  communication guidelines, 38,
      39
  professional standards, 38
  and risk terminology, 16
  SAS 61, 38
  SAS 112, 38
"Amount" versus "number," 105
Analytical method of report
      organization, 74
Annual internal control report,
      32, 174
Apostrophes, 135, 136

Appendices
  backup documentation, 59
  and detailed data, 74
  use of, 19
Asia, communication issues, 152
Atkinson, Cliff, 129
Audience
  analyzing, 152–157
  informal surveys and
      preferences, 96
Audit committees
  Auditor Reports to Audit
      Committees (SOX Section
      204), 31, 172
  expanded role of, 20
  report format preferences, 06
Audit components
  collaboration on, 13–15
  noncompliance, disclosure of,
      14
  traditional, 14, 15
Audit process
  collaboration, 10, 13–15, 22,
      76, 77, 152
  communication skills required,
      11–23. See also
      Communication
  core issues, deciding on, 1
      5, 16

Audit process *(Cont.)*
　documentation, 3, 36, 37,
　　203–210
　executive summary, 22, 23, 57,
　　59
　first meeting, 11–13
　flowchart, 6, 7, 9
　information to include, deciding
　　on, 16–19
　linking (synthesis thinking),
　　19–21, 36
　listening skills, 11–13. *See also*
　　Listening skills
　revision and rewriting, 21, 22.
　　See also Editing
Audit request form, use of, 13
Audit trails and advantages of
　automation, 45
Auditors
　and advantages of automation,
　　46
　Certified Information Systems
　　Auditor (CISA), 52
　communication. *See*
　　Communication
　and IT audits, 50–52
　knowledge and expertise, 45,
　　52, 181, 182
　report to audit committee, 31,
　　172
　role of, 218
Automation
　advantages of, 44–47
　and audit reports, 43
　business English, 75
　challenges, 47–50
　importing text, 58
　and need for writing, 91
　and report format, 57–59
　and Sarbanes-Oxley, 44

BBI Group, 20
Brody, Richard, 17
Brown, John Seely, 149

Capitalization, 138, 139
Causes as traditional audit
　component, 15
Certified Information Systems
　Auditor (CISA), 52
Checklists
　audience analysis, 154
　IT reports, 50, 51
Chief Audit Executives (CAEs), 2
Chief executive officer (CEO)
　certification of financial reports
　　and disclosures, 32, 91,
　　172–174
　responsibilities, 217
Chief financial officer (CFO)
　certification of financial reports
　　and disclosures, 32, 91,
　　172–174
　responsibilities, 217
Clarity, writing standards,
　28–30
COBIT/COSO, 156
Collaboration
　on audit plan, 13, 14
　and deciding on core issues, 15
　importance of, 76, 77, 152
　need for, 10
　and rewriting process, 22
Colons, 136
Commas, 135–137. *See also*
　Punctuation
　and editing process, 146
　sample sentences with
　　errors and corrections,
　　226–228
Committee of Sponsoring
　Organizations of the
　Treadway Commission
　(COSO), Integrated
　Framework for Internal
　Controls
　generally, 2, 39, 40
　provisions of, 211–221
　voluntary compliance with, 151

Communication
AICPA guidelines, 38, 39
and audience analysis, 96,
 152–157
and audit documentation, 36
and audit process, 6
auditors and IT, 49–52
collaborative, 152
COSO framework for internal
 controls, 39, 40, 214
deficiencies and material
 weaknesses, 200–202
duty to communicate
 engagement results, 1, 170,
 171
e-mail, 85–89
and essential versus nonessential
 information, 16–19
graphics, use of. *See* Graphics
informal discussions, 76, 77
Institute of Internal Auditors
 (IIA) standards, 26–28, 78,
 170, 171
interpretation of information,
 12, 13
linking (synthesis thinking),
 19–21, 36
listening skills, 11–12, 15, 78,
 79, 154, 155
need for, 10, 11
on-the-job talking (OJT), 77
oral, 78, 80, 82, 83
PCAOB Auditing Standard No.
 2, 35, 200–203
positive versus combative
 conversation, 82, 83
probing for information. *See*
 Probes
Sarbanes-Oxley implications,
 31–33
SAS 61, Auditor's
 Communication with Those
 Charged with Governance,
 38

shared interpretations, 77
telephone, 83–85
tips and techniques, 79
and walkthroughs, 82
Comparative method of report
 organization, 74
Completeness
executive certification of, 32,
 91, 172–174
as writing standard, 28, 30
Comprehensive audit reporting
 process. *See* Audit process
Computer Sciences Corporation,
 10
Conciseness
achieving, 107–111
as writing standard, 28, 30
Conclusions
and executive summary, 23
IIA communication standards,
 26
Conditions as audit component,
 15
Connectedthinking, 21
Consistency, checking for, 145
Constructiveness as writing
 standard, 28, 30
Core issues, 15, 16
Corporate responsibility for
 financial reports, 31, 32,
 172–174
Cover letter, 59
Criteria, as traditional audit
 component, 15
Cultural comparison, 152–154
Currencies, 159

Data analysis
and advantages of automation,
 47
filtering data, 48
Data definition, 12
Data gathering, 6, 20
Data synthesis, 20, 21

"Data" versus "information," 105
Deductive approach, data
    synthesis, 20, 21
Deference, 82, 83
Deficiencies, 16, 177, 178
Diamond, Irv, 156
Disclosure of noncompliance, 14,
    171
Distribution of results, 27, 28
Diversity, 152
Documentation, PCAOB Auditing
    Standard No. 3, 23, 36, 37,
    203–210
Duguid, Paul, 149
Duty to communicate engagement
    results, 1

E-mail communication
    brevity, 85, 86
    examples, 86–88
    recipients of, limiting, 85
    tips and techniques, 89
Editing
    active voice, 147
    adverbs, 146
    commas, 146. *See also* Commas
    executive summary, 23
    graphic continuity, 145
    misplaced modifiers, 147
    paragraph structure, 147
    as part of writing process, 22
    punctuation, 146
    reading aloud, 148
    reading backward, 147
    and reliance on spellcheckers,
        144, 145
    subject/verb agreement, 146. *See
        also* Verbs
    tips and techniques, 145
    use of -ion and -ment words,
        146
Effective writing, tips and
    techniques for, 93

Effects, as traditional audit
    component, 15
Enron, 162
Enterprise Risk Management
    (ERM), 2
Event-driven companies, 10
Excel
    accuracy of spreadsheets, 47
    and report formats, 58, 59
    tables and graphics tools,
        use of, 141
    use of, 21
Executive summary
    automated formats, 57
    as part of report, 22, 23
    and reader expectations, 59
Executives
    certification of accuracy and
        completeness of financial
        reports, 32, 91, 172–174
Expletives, 109, 110

Few, Stephen, 141
Filtering of information and
    data analysis, 48
Financial institution audit report
    template, 66–71
Financial reports, Corporate
    Responsibility for (SOX
    Section 302), 31, 32,
    172–174
Flowchart, audit process, 6, 7, 9
Follow-up inquiries, 82
Footnotes, 142
Foreign Corrupt Practices Act,
    156
Format of reports
    appendices, 19, 59, 74
    audit committee preferences,
        96
    and automation, 57–59
    basic principles, 60
    expectations, 59, 60

financial institution audit report
template, 66–71
guidelines, 59
headings and subheadings, 75
internal audit report template,
61–65
IT management deficiency
report template, 72, 73
organizational methods, 74
spacing, 75
style guides, 40, 59
Table of Contents (TOC), 13,
59, 96, 145
tables, 74, 75, 141, 142
tabular, 57, 58, 74, 131
Functional method of report
organization, 74

Gallagher, Robert F., 162
Garbage-in, garbage-out,
47, 91
Generalities, avoiding, 104, 105
Generally Accepted Accounting
Principles (GAAP), 156
Generally Accepted Auditing
Standards (GAAS), 181
Gill, Jasvir, 27
Girard, Stephane, 27, 155
Global Integrator, 152–154
Global issues. *See* Multinational
organizations
Grammar
active voice, 100, 101, 109
and global use of English
language, 157–158
modern rules, 98, 99
modifiers, 123, 124, 146, 147,
158, 224–226
nouns, 138, 146
parallel structure, 103, 104,
118, 119
sentence structure. *See* Sentence
structure

subject and verb agreement, 99,
100
verbs. *See* Verbs
Graphics
and appearance of report, 140,
141
footnotes, 142
graphic continuity, 145
graphs, 143, 144
tables, 74, 75, 141, 142
tips and techniques, 143, 144
Graphs, 143, 144

Headings and subheadings, 75
Higher-order thinking skills
(HOTS), 19–21, 131
Homonyms, 158
HOTS. *See* Higher-order thinking
skills (HOTS)
Hyphens, 138

IBM mainframes, System
Management Facility (SMF)
reference guide, 51
Impact as traditional audit
component, 14
India
and CISA designation, 52
and use of English language,
157, 158
Inductive approach, data
gathering, 20
Information
data compared, 105
gathering, use of probes, 35,
80–83
Information technology (IT)
and accounting, 47, 48
audit tips and techniques, 52
auditors' knowledge of, 45, 52,
169
communication with auditors,
49–52

Information technology *(Cont.)*
  and impact of Sarbanes-Oxley, 43, 44
  mainframes, 51
  management deficiency report template, 72, 73
  operating systems, 50
  and report production process, 3
  and risk criteria, 16
  security issues, 48, 49
Institute of Internal Auditors (IIA)
  Attribute Standard 1200, 169
  communication standards, 26–28, 78
  internal auditors, IT knowledge and expertise, 45, 52, 169
  International Standards for the Professional Practice of Internal Auditing, Introduction, 167–169
  and need for standards, 25, 26
  Performance Standard 2100, 170
  Performance Standard 2400, 170, 171
  and report formats, 59
  as source of standards, 2
  writing standards, 28–31
Internal audit report template, 61–65
Internal control
  annual internal control report, 32, 174
  COSO framework, 39, 40, 211–221
  Management Assessment of Internal Controls (SOX Section 404), 31–33, 174
  and media reports, 161, 162
  over financial reporting, 176, 177

PCAOB Auditing Standard No. 2, 34, 35, 175–203
SEC regulations, 33, 34
International audit reporting. *See* Multinational organizations
IT. *See* Information technology (IT)
ITIL, 156

Jeffery, B.L., 51

Kissinger, Henry, 155

Lack of subordination, 109
Lefton, Robert E., 81
Linking (synthesis thinking), 19–21, 36
Listening skills
  active listening, 11, 12
  and deciding core issues, 15
  and global communication, 154, 155
  need for, 78, 79
  tips and techniques, 12
Logic, and report writing, 5

Mainframes, 51
Management
  assessment of internal controls, SOX requirement, 31–33
  by exception, 10
Mansfield, Paul, 88
Materiality
  essential versus nonessential information, 17
  material weakness, 35, 38, 175, 178, 179, 200, 201
  terminology, 16
Media reports, 161, 162
Meetings, documentation of, 11
Microsoft Excel
  accuracy of spreadsheets, 47
  and report formats, 58, 59
  tables and graphics tools, use of, 141

Minutes of meetings, 11
Modifiers
  adverbs, 146
  defined, 123
  irregular comparative forms of
    adjectives, 158
  misplaced, 123, 124, 147
  sample sentences with errors
    and corrections, 224–226
Movado Group, The, 27
Multinational organizations
  audience analysis, 152–157
  and audit reporting, 155–157
  currencies, indicating, 159
  English language, use of, 157,
    158
  and Sarbanes-Oxley compliance,
    151

Narrative report format, 15, 16,
    74
Nici, Joe, 27
Noncompliance disclosure, 14,
    171
Nouns
  hyphenated words, 138
  verbs made into, 101, 102,
    146

Objectives of audit
  and audit request forms,
    12, 13
  and determination of relevant
    information, 18
  engagement objectives, 15, 175,
    176
  and listening skills, 11
  risk identification, 2, 185
Objectivity as writing standard,
    28, 39
Operating systems, 50
Oracle, 48
Oral reports, 1

Order of importance method of
  report organization, 74
Organization, 36
Outlines, review of by report
  recipients, 96

Paragraphs
  guidelines, 130, 131
  topic sentences, 131, 132, 147
  transitions, 132–134
Parallel structure, 38, 103, 104,
    118, 119
PCAOB. *See* Public Company
  Accounting Oversight Board
  (PCAOB)
Planning, and role of internal
  auditors,
    10, 11, 183, 184
Prepositions and prepositional
  phrases, 110, 124–126
Preventive versus detective
  controls, 43, 179
  and advantages of automation,
    46, 47
Pricewaterhouse Coopers, 21
Probes
  importance of, 81, 82
  as method of discovering
    information, 80
  positive, 83
  types of, 81, 82
  use of, 35
Process-driven reporting
  described, 7, 8, 10, 11
Processes, 10, 195, 196
Public Company Accounting
  Oversight Board (PCAOB)
  Auditing Standard No. 2,
    internal control, 34, 35,
    175–203
  Auditing Standard No. 3, Audit
    Documentation, 23, 36, 37,
    203–210

Public Company Accounting
    Oversight Board *(Cont.)*
  guidance from, 10
  inquiries and follow-up
      questions, importance
      of, 82
  purpose of, 34
  quality over quantity directive,
      37
  as source of standards, 2
Punctuation
  apostrophes, 135, 136
  colons, 136
  commas, 135–137, 146
  and editing process, 146
  hyphens, 138
  importance of, 129, 130, 134
  sample sentences with errors
      and corrections, 226–228
  semicolons, 137

Qualifiers, use of, 110
Quality over quantity directive, 37

Ramos, Michael, 16
Ranadive, Vivek, 10
Readability, rules for, 40, 41
Real-time information and
    action, 10
Reasons, as traditional audit
    component, 14
Recommendations, as traditional
    audit component, 15
Redundancy, 108
Release of engagement results,
    Institute
    of Internal Auditors (IIA)
    standards, 27
Relevance, 6
  essential versus nonessential
      information, 16–19
  significant findings or issues, 36,
      37

Repetition, 108
Report writing
  audit notification as beginning
      of, 6
  automated. *See* Automation
  as computer programming, 5, 6
  data gathering, 6, 20
  effective writing tips and
      techniques, 93
  flowchart, 8
  format. *See* Format of reports
  "whatever" step, 111, 112
  word choice. *See* Word
      choice
  writer's block, 159–161
  writing as decision-making
      process, 95
"Respectively," use of term, 104
Rewrites. *See* Editing
Risk
  assessment, 2, 8, 185
  categorizing, 2
  criteria, 16
  management, 170
  terminology, 16
Rogers, Will, 105
Rosenberg, Marshall, 83

SAP, 27
Sarbanes-Oxley (SOX)
  collaboration requirement, 10
  costs of compliance, 151
  goals of, 152
  impact of, 27, 151, 152, 161
  impact on internal audit
      profession, 150, 151
  and integrity of corporate data,
      43, 44
  internal controls reporting, 44
  provisions of, 172–174
  reporting process, 2
  reports required, 1
  risk, categorizing, 2

Section 204, Auditor Reports to
Audit Committees, 31, 32,
172
Section 302, Corporate
Responsibility for Financial
Reports, 31, 32, 172–174
Section 404, Management
Assessment of Internal
Controls, 31–33, 174
as source of standards, 2
standards for report
writing, 25
voluntary compliance
with, 151
Schertzer, Margaret, 135
Schlumberger Ltd., 27
Scope of audit, 15
Scrutiny of written reports, 1
Securities and Exchange
Commission (SEC), 10
internal control over financial
reporting, 33, 34
materiality terminology, 16
Security issues, information
technology, 48, 49
Segregation of duties, 48
Semicolons, 137
Senko, Ted, 150
Sentence components
active voice, 119, 120
coherence, 117
parallelism, 103, 104, 118, 119
predicate, 115
single idea, 116, 117
subject, 114–116
variety, 117, 118
Sentence structure
components of sentence,
114–120
examples of poor sentences
and corrected versions,
126, 127
importance of, 113, 114

modifiers, 123, 124
predicate, 115
prepositions, 124–126
run-on sentences, 114
sentence schemata (diagrams),
use of, 120–122
subject identification,
114–116
Significant deficiencies, 35, 38,
178, 200, 201
Significant findings or issues, 36,
37, 209, 210
Software. *See also* Automation
and international audit
reporting, 156
Statistical Analysis Systems
(SAS), 44, 50
Spellcheckers, 144, 145
Spencer-Pickett, K.H., 49
Spreadsheets
accuracy, 47
and report formats, 58, 59
tables and graphics tools,
use of, 141
use of, 21
Standards
AICPA professional standards,
38, 39
as audit component, 14
company standards, 40
COSO framework for internal
controls, 2, 39, 40, 211–221
Institute of Internal Auditors
(IIA), 26–31, 78,
167–171
Public Company Accounting
Oversight Board (PCAOB),
2, 23, 34–37, 175–210
readability, 40, 41
Sarbanes-Oxley, implications of,
25, 31–33
SEC regulations, 33, 34
sources of, 2

Statements of Auditing Standards (SAS)
  and Sarbanes-Oxley, 44
  SAS 61, 38
  SAS 112, 38
Statistical Analysis Systems (SAS)
    software, 44
  and auditors' IT requests, 50
Steinberg, Richard M., 106
Sternberg, Sy, 162
Stevens, Bill, 20
Story structure, 129
Style guides, 40, 59
Swiss Consulting Group, The, 152
Synthesis thinking (linking),
    19–21, 36

Table of Contents (TOC)
  audit plan, relation to, 13
  early review of by report
    recipients, 96
  and graphic continuity, 145
  and reader expectations, 59
Tables, 74, 75, 141, 142
Telephone communication
  effective use of, 84
  messages, 84
  shortcomings of, 83
  tips and techniques, 85
Terminology
  risk criteria, 16
  and use of definitions, 106
Terms of Reference (TOR)
    document, 11
Timeliness, as writing standard,
    28, 31
"Too much information" (TMI),
    16, 57
Topic sentences, 131, 132, 147
Transition words, 132–134
Transparency, 6
Tufte, Edward R., 141, 143, 144
Typos, 147

United Kingdom
  American English versus British
    English, 157
  collective nouns as plurals, 100
  and word choice, 97

Verbs
  active versus passive voice, 100,
    101, 147
  and hyphenated words, 138
  irregular, 158
  making into nouns, 101, 102,
    146
  and parallel structure, 103,
    104, 118, 119
  and predicate, 115
  sample sentences with errors
    and corrections, 222–224
  and sentence structure. *See*
    Sentence structure
  subject agreement, 99, 100,
    146
  tenses, 102, 103
Vidal, Gore, 155

Walkthroughs, 82, 197–199
Wensberg, Eric, 123
White space, use of, 75, 131, 141
Word choice
  acronyms, use of, 58, 105, 106
  audience consideration, 95, 96
  conciseness, 107–111
  criteria, 95–99
  generally accepted business
    usage, 96–98
  grammar. *See* Grammar
  precise and specific words,
    104–107
  terminology and use of
    definitions, 106
  "whatever" step, 111, 112
Wordiness, 109
Writer's block, 58, 159–161

Writing standards
  accuracy, 28, 29
  clarity, 28–30
  complete, 28, 30
  concise, 28, 30
  constructive, 28, 30
  Institute of Internal Auditors
    (IIA) standards, 28–31
  objectivity, 28, 29
  timeliness, 28, 31

Writing style, 75
  audit committee preferences,
    96
  and making verbs into nouns,
    101, 102
  tips and techniques, 97, 98
Wurman, Richard Saul, 157

Zinsser, William, 92, 98
Zweifel, Thomas, 155